Photo: Don Russel

The Art of the Band Saw
Award-Winning Designs

Scarab Chairs by David J. Marks,
wenge and maple, 37^1/$_2$" high x 24" wide x 24" deep

The Art of the Band Saw
Award-Winning Designs

Mark Duginske

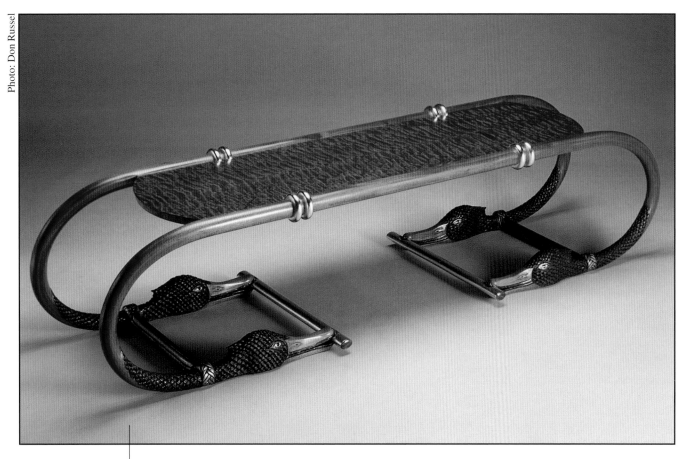

Ancient Egyptian-inspired Table by David J. Marks,
quilted mahogany, Honduran mahogany, and ebony,
16" high x 18" wide x 71" long

Sterling Publishing Co., Inc. New York
A Sterling / Chapelle Book

Chapelle:

Jo Packham, Owner

Cathy Sexton, Editor

Staff: Ann Bear, Areta Bingham, Kass Burchett, Marilyn Goff, Holly Hollingsworth, Susan Jorgensen, Barbara Milburn, Linda Orton, Karmen Quinney, Leslie Ridenour, Cindy Stoeckl, Gina Swapp, Sara Toliver

Photography: Various professional photographers unknown by name, unless indicated.
Photo on Cover: *Chair by Brian Boggs*
Photo on page 1:
   Glass Top Dining Table by David J. Marks, Burmese padauk and Brazilian rosewood, 30" high x 46" wide x 74" long

If you have any questions or comments or would like information on specialty products featured in this book, please contact Chapelle, Ltd., Inc., P.O. Box 9252, Ogden, UT 84409 • (801) 621-2777 • (801) 621-2788 Fax • e-mail: chapelle@chapelleltd.com • website: www.chapelleltd.com

Library of Congress Cataloging-in-Publication Data

Duginske, Mark.
        The art of the band saw : award-winning designs / Mark Duginske.
             p.   cm.
        "A Sterling/Chapelle book."
        Includes index.
        ISBN 0-8069-3891-9
        1. Band saws. 2. Woodwork. I. Title.
    TT186.D838 2001
    684'.083--dc21   2001020915

10 9 8 7 6 5 4 3 2 1

Published by Sterling Publishing Company, Inc.
387 Park Avenue South, New York, NY 10016
© 2001 by Mark Duginske
Distributed in Canada by Sterling Publishing
c/o Canadian Manda Group, One Atlantic Avenue, Suite 105
Toronto, Ontario, Canada M6K 3E7
Distributed in Great Britain and Europe by Cassell PLC
Wellington House, 125 Strand, London WC2R 0BB, England
Distributed in Australia by Capricorn Link (Australia) Pty Ltd.
P.O. Box 704, Windsor, NSW 2756 Australia
Printed and Bound in China
All Rights Reserved

Sterling ISBN 0-8069-3891-9

about the author

"The Little Drummer Boy" by Ken Frye, pear, 48" high x 16" wide x 12½" deep

MARK DUGINSKE is a fourth-generation central-Wisconsin woodworker. He makes his living as a woodworker, designer, writer, and inventor.

He was formerly a contributing editor to *Fine Woodworking Magazine* and now writes for a number of magazines. His work has appeared in *Fine Woodworking, American Woodworker, Fine Home Building, The Design Book, Americana, Chicago Magazine, Architectural Digest, Architectural Record, Woodsmith, Wood Shop News,* and *Wood News.*

His restoration work in the Frank Lloyd Wright Home and Studio in Oak Park, Illinois, has appeared on *This Old House* and the PBS *Frank Lloyd Wright Special.*

He is the author of nine books and has five patents.

A SPECIAL THANKS TO:

DAVID WELTER, College of the Redwoods

RICHARD GOTZ, Minnesota Woodworkers Guild

contents

band saw fundamentals

The band saw is named after the type of blade that is used on the saw. This blade is a continuous metal band with teeth on one side. It is suspended over two or three metal wheels. As the wheels rotate, so does the blade, creating the cutting action.

The band saw is one of the most frequently used power tools in the workshop. Though it is often used for cutting wood, it can be used to cut other materials, such as most metals and a variety of plastics.

It is also considered the safest of the power tools. Because the direction of the blade is always downward, there is no danger that the wood will be thrown back at the operator, which is called kickback.

The most unique feature of the band saw is that the workpiece can be rotated around the blade, creating a curve as shown in Illus. 1-1.

It is the tool most often used when cutting curves in wood. By using a narrow blade such as a $1/16"$, the workpiece can easily be rotated around the blade, creating tight scrollwork as shown in Illus. 1-2.

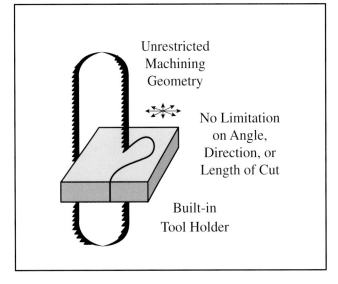

Illus. 1-1. The blade used on a band saw is a continuous metal band with teeth on one side. One unique feature of the band saw is that the workpiece can be rotated around the blade, creating a curve. The band saw is considered a safe tool to use because the blade has a downward cutting motion. It holds the workpiece on the table.

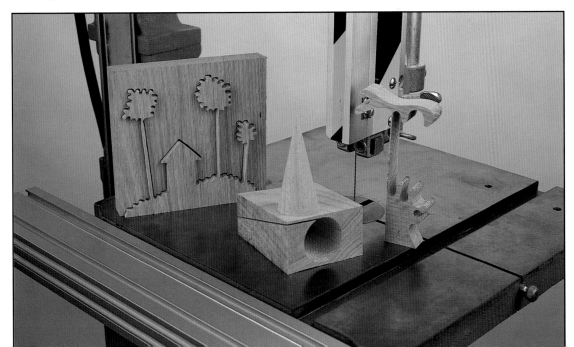

Illus. 1-2. The $1/16"$ blade gives a smooth finish in a multi-grain cut. As the blade dulls, the finish becomes smoother. Fine blades last for a fairly long time when cutting oak or other woods which do not contain pitch.

Because the band saw blade is fairly thin, it can cut thick stock with a minimum of horsepower. For this reason, the band saw is often used when thick pieces of wood have to be cut or when valuable pieces of wood are made into thin pieces of veneer.

Parts of the Band Saw

The band saw is a simple machine which does not have many parts. Although each manufacturer makes a slightly different machine, they are basically the same as shown in Illus. 1-3.

If you are not familiar with the band saw, take the time to study the illustration below as it relates to your particular machine. Make certain to read your owner's manual. For more information we suggest the book *Band Saw Workshop Bench Reference*.

• Top and Bottom Wheels

The blade is suspended over the top and bottom wheels. As they rotate, the blade also rotates, creating the downward cutting action. The wheels are usually covered with a piece of rubber called a tire. The tire cushions the blade and protects the teeth from coming into contact with the metal wheels.

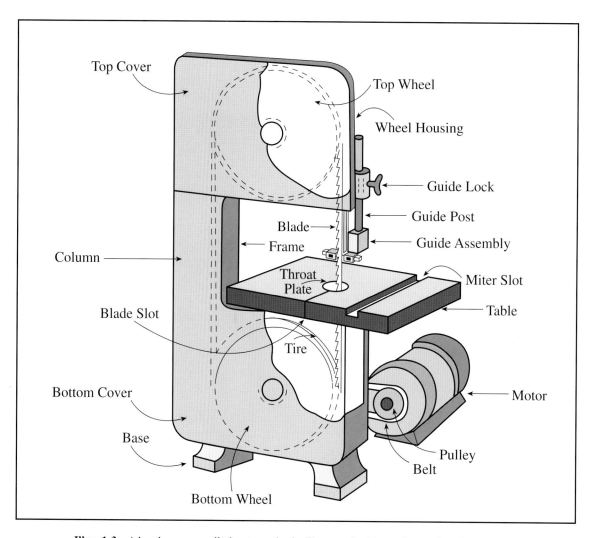

Illus. 1-3. A band saw generally has two wheels. The top wheel is used to track and tension the ·blade. The bottom wheel powers the blade and pulls it downward through the workpiece.

The top wheel performs two functions. The first function is balancing, or tracking, the blade on the wheels. An adjustable tilt mechanism is used to balance the blade. The second function is tensioning the blade. The wheel moves up or down increasing the tension of the blade. These functions are described in Chapter 2.

The bottom wheel is the drive wheel. It is attached to the power source either directly or with a belt. The bottom wheel powers the blade and pulls it downward through the workpiece.

• Frame

Most of the important parts of the band saw, including the wheels and table, are attached to the frame. There are various styles of frames and each manufacturer makes the frame differently. Skeletal frames are simply frameworks that are either cast or welded.

A separate piece of sheet metal is often attached to the frame to safely cover the back of the saw. This protective cover is called a wheel housing.

• Top and Bottom Covers

Top and bottom covers protect the operator from the wheels and the blade. If the blade breaks, the pieces of blade are contained by the covers.

The covers are either of one or two pieces: some are hinged; some are attached with knobs or clips. The two most common materials used for covers are plastic and metal. Plastic is quieter and less susceptible to vibration. Because of vibration, metal covers should be secured tightly to avoid noise.

• Table

The workpiece rests on the table as it is fed into the blade. The table surrounds the blade. A large hole in the middle of the table around the blade allows the operator to make adjustments below the table. This hole is covered by the throat plate. A slot in the table allows the blade entry into the middle of the table.

The table on most band saws is designed to tilt, which means that it can make beveled or angled cuts. The table tilts away from the column up to 45°. On some models, it also tilts toward the column up to 10°. It is most useful for cutting dovetail pins. This added feature may be handy at times, but it is not a necessity.

Beneath the table is an adjustable bolt or screw to help level the table back to 90° after the table has been tilted. These functions are described in Chapter 8.

A scale and a pointer register the angle of the tilt. The pointer and the leveling bolt should be adjusted to an accurate 90°. The best way to do this is to use an accurate square as shown in Illus. 1-4.

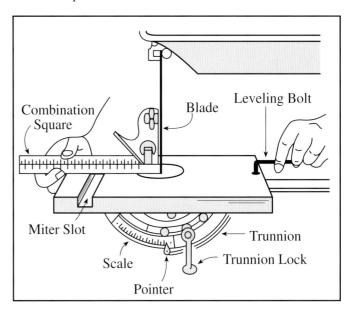

Illus. 1-4. The parts of a typical band saw table. Check often to make certain the table is square to the blade.

• Miter Slot

Most saws have a miter slot which is a groove in the table that runs parallel to the blade and accepts the miter guide, which is usually used for crosscutting (cutting across the grain of the wood). The miter slot is very useful for owner-built jigs, which are described in Chapters 7 and 8. Many jigs are designed to operate parallel to the blade and the miter slot provides the most logical path.

• Guide Assembly

There are two guide assemblies which support the blade. One is located below the table and one above the table. The top assembly is attached to a metal rod called the guide post. The entire upper guide assembly is adjustable up and down so it can be adjusted just above the workpiece as shown in Illus. 1-5.

The blade guard is attached to the front of the guide post. Each guide assembly consists of two guide blocks that are located on each side of the blade and keep it from twisting. Each assembly also houses the thrust bearing, which keeps the blade from being pushed rearward when the saw is cutting as shown in Illus. 1-6.

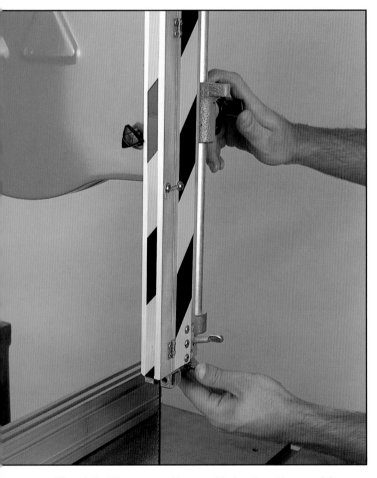

Illus. 1-5. The upper guide assembly is adjustable up and down. The blade guard is attached to the front of the assembly. A blade guard protects the operator from the blade. For safety and performance reasons, lock the assembly approximately $1/4$" above the workpiece.

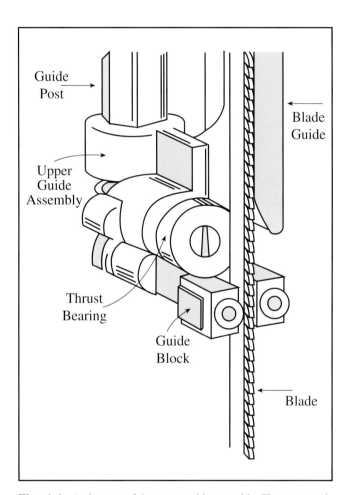

Illus. 1-6. A close-up of the upper guide assembly. The upper and lower guide assembly is a casting that holds the bearings and the guide holder.

safety procedures

The band saw is a popular tool because it is easy to use and because it is so versatile.
It is also fairly safe to use. However, you should not take this for granted.

Read the following safety rules carefully and strictly observe each one.

- When using any power tool, make certain to wear eye and ear protection at all times.

- Before using any tool, make certain to carefully read and follow all manufacturer's safety guidelines.

- When using any power tool, never wear loose articles of clothing.

- When using a band saw, make certain the guards are in place and use them at all times. The guards protect you from coming in contact with the blade.

- When using a band saw, make certain the saw blade teeth point downward toward the table.

- When using a band saw, adjust the upper blade guard so that it is about $^1/_4''$ above the material being sawn.

- When using a band saw, make certain the blade has been properly tensioned and tracked.

- When using a band saw, make certain to stop the machine before removing the scrap pieces from the table.

- When using any saw, always keep your hands and fingers away from the blade.

- When using any saw, make certain to use the proper size and type of blade.

- When using a band saw, hold the workpiece firmly against the table. Do not attempt to saw stock that does not have a flat surface, unless a suitable support is used.

- When using a band saw, use a push stick at the end of a cut. This is the most dangerous time because the cut is complete and the blade is exposed. Push sticks are available commercially.

- When using a band saw, hold the wood firmly and feed it into the blade at a moderate speed.

- When using a band saw, turn off the machine if you have to back the material out of an incomplete or jammed cut.

adjustment and alignment

For you to get the best performance from your saw, it must be properly tuned and adjusted. Adjustment includes tracking and tensioning the blades and then adjusting the thrust-bearing guides and guide posts.

Any band saw that is not properly adjusted works poorly and can be frustrating to use. Having a well-tuned and adjusted band saw in your shop has many benefits. It will greatly increase your confidence and your cutting options. It makes the woodworking more efficient and enjoyable.

Finally, a well-tuned band saw can prevent accidents. You can rip small pieces that are dangerous to cut on table or radial arm saws. All the attention you give it is certainly worth the effort.

The following is an examination of each of the procedures for tuning your saw.

Blade Tracking

The term "tracking" refers to the act of positioning or balancing the band saw blade on the wheels. Every time you put a new or different blade on the saw, you have to track it. There is no external force that holds the blade on the wheel. It is held on by a combination of two factors. One factor is the outside shape of the wheel. The second factor is the angle of the top wheel.

• Wheel Shape

The shape of the wheel is determined by the shape of the metal casting on the rim of the wheel. The outside rim of the wheel is covered with a piece of rubber called a tire, which is between $1/8"$ and $1/4"$ thick. The tire acts as a cushion and a shock absorber.

Wheels are either flat or curved. The curved shape is called a crown. The crown exerts a controlling force on the blade which causes it to ride near the middle, but not in the exact middle, of the wheel.

The disadvantage of a crowned wheel is that it provides minimal surface area between the blade and the tire. This makes it more difficult to track large blades such as a $1/2"$ blade, which is the best blade to use for straight cuts, especially resawing. If the crowned wheels are not perfectly aligned with each other, the crowns on each wheel will compete for control of the blade. This causes vibration and shortens the life of a blade.

When the tire starts to wear, a depression forms in the tire and makes the blades harder to track. You can alleviate this by dressing the tires with sandpaper so that there is a crown of about .020" or the thickness of five pieces of paper.

• Top Wheel Angle

The second factor that affects the tracking of a blade is the angle of the top wheel. The angle of the top wheel steers the blade in the direction of the tilt as shown in Illus. 2-1 on opposite page. The usual approach is to tilt the top wheel, usually rearward, until the blade tracks in the center of the top wheel. This approach is the one that is usually recommended in the owner's manual. It is called "center tracking."

Center tracking works well on blades that are $3/16"$ wide or narrower. These blades are flexible, and the misalignment of the wheel does not harm the performance or the life expectancy of the blades. However, larger blades, those wider than $1/4"$, are not flexible like the narrower blades. Track these wider blades with the wheels lined up with each other, rather than with the top wheel angled. This is called "coplanar tracking"

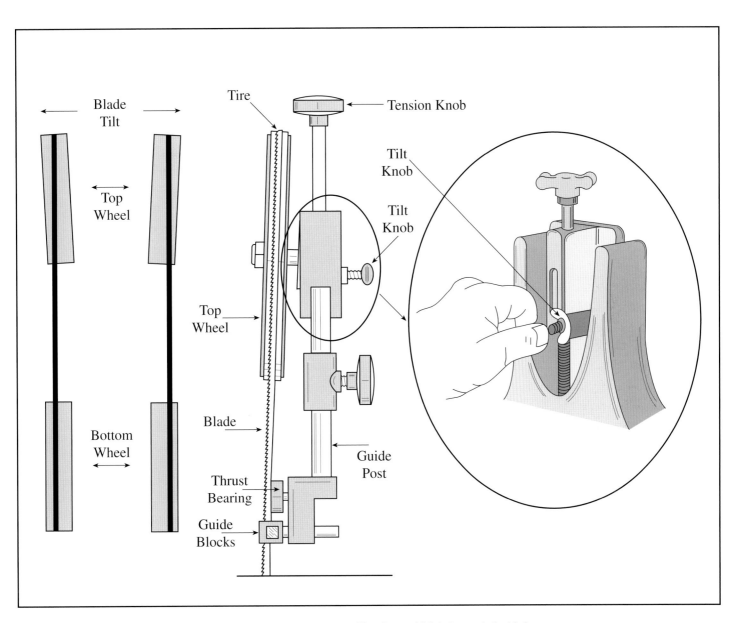

Illus. 2-1. The crown exerts a controlling force which helps track the blade near the center of the wheel. The angle of the top wheel steers the blade in the direction of the tilt. A knob on the back of the saw tilts the top wheel. When center tracking, angle the top wheel by turning the knob until the blade tracks in the middle of it. Use center tracking on blades that are $^3/_{16}$" wide or narrower.

because the wheels are in a coplanar position (lying in the same plane) as shown in Illus. 2-2.

If the wheels are coplanar, the blade will find its own equilibrium and essentially track itself. One of the things you will notice when you are using coplanar tracking is that the blade will have a tendency to track toward the front of the wheels. The reason why this area is the position of equilibrium is because the front of the blade is shorter than the back of the blade. When the blade is manufactured, the teeth are first ground and then hardened, which causes the front of the blade to shrink in relationship to the back.

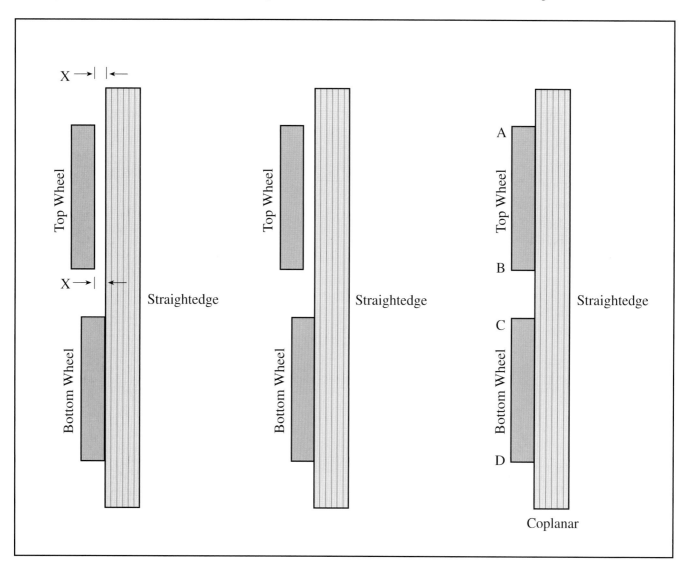

Illus. 2-2. Coplanar wheels lie in the same plane. The first step in coplanar tracking is aligning the wheels with the straightedge. Use coplanar tracking on blades that are $1/4$" wide or wider. The straight edge should touch the top and bottom of both wheels.

Tracking Procedure

If you use a consistent step-by-step method, tracking should take only a minute or two. Be careful when using blades, especially wide and sharp ones. Some people prefer to use gloves when handling large blades. Safety glasses are always advised. Following are the step-by-step procedures for tracking a blade.

• Installing the Blade

1. Loosen the guides on the side of the blade and then retract them. This way, you can easily install the next blade without having any obstructions.

2. Uncoil the blade. Remember to use gloves and safety glasses. If it is a new blade, it may have oil or dirt on it. The blade may have been oiled to prevent rust. You do not want the oil or dirt touching the workpiece, so wipe the blade off with a rag or a paper towel before installing it. Pull the blade through the rag rearward so the teeth do not catch the rag.

3. If the teeth are pointed in the wrong direction, you will have to turn the blade inside out. To do this, hold the blade with both hands and rotate it.

4. Slide it through the table slot and place it on the wheels. Some people prefer to hang it from the top wheel, taking advantage of the force of gravity.

5. Position the blade where you want it on the wheels. Then tension it (make it taut between the wheels). Slowly raise the top wheel with the tension knob. Start to rotate the wheels by hand in the normal direction while the blade is still fairly slack. As you do this, watch to determine where the blade wants to track. If the blade is tracking too far forward or backward, make an adjustment with the tilt mechanism. As you rotate the blade with one hand, increase its tension, or tautness, with the other as shown in Illus. 2-3. Continue to do this until you have adequate tension.

A blade cannot be correctly tracked until the tensioning is completed. Never track the blade with the saw running.

6. After the blade has been tracked, replace the cover and the blade guard. Plug in the electrical cord. Turn the saw on for a few seconds and then turn it off again. Watch to see how the saw runs. If the blade seems to track well, run it under full power. Following are the specific tracking instructions.

Illus. 2-3. When you tension the blade, rotate the top wheel at the same time. Check the blade tracking as the tension increases. Here a $1/2$"-wide blade is being tensioned on a Delta band saw.

• Tracking Small Blades

If you are using *center tracking* (best for $1/16$" to $3/16$" blades) rotate the wheel by hand and angle the top wheel until the blade is tracking in the middle of the top wheel. Make several revolutions of the blade to make certain that the blade stays in the same place on the wheels. Lock the tilt knob. Center tracking works best on blades that are $3/16$" wide and narrower. If you are using large blades, *coplanar tracking* works best.

• Tracking Large Blades

Align the wheels with a straightedge after tensioning the large blade. The largest blade most saws can handle is $1/2$". Make several revolutions of the blade to make certain that it stays in the same place on the wheels. The blade may or may not track in the center of the top wheel. The blade will usually track toward the front of the wheels. Lock the tilt knob. Tilt the top wheel slightly rearward if the blade starts to move forward or comes off the front of the saw. Coplanar tracking works best with blades that are $1/4$" wide and wider.

Adjusting the Band Saw

Parts of the band saw must be adjusted so the band saw can make accurate cuts. You should be aware of how they function before you learn to adjust them.

As the workpiece is moved into the blade, a mechanism is needed to prevent the blade from being shoved off the wheels. On most saws, a round wheel bearing called the "thrust bearing" is used to stop the rearward movement of the blade as shown in Illus. 2-4. There are usually two thrust bearings, one above and one below the table.

"Guides" are paired with each thrust bearing on each side of the blade. The guides prevent the sideways movement, or deflection, of the blade. They also prevent excessive twisting of the blade when it is being used to cut curves.

There are usually four guides, one on each side of the blade above and below the table. The guides and

bearing are held in place by a metal casting called the "guide assembly." There are two guide assemblies: one above and one below the table. The top guide assembly is attached to the guide post, which is movable up and down and is thus adjustable to the thickness of the workpiece.

Each guide assembly has a mechanism for the independent forward and rearward movement of the guides and thrust bearing. This guide assembly design accommodates different blade widths.

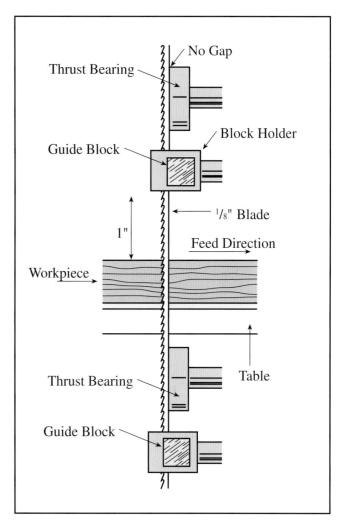

Illus. 2-4. The thrust bearing is located behind the blade and prevents the blade from being shoved rearward by the workpiece. The guides are located on each side of the blade and prevent twisting and deflecting.

Adjusting the Guide Post

The top guide assembly is attached to a movable post that is raised or lowered to accommodate different thicknesses of wood. The post should be adjusted so that there is about $1/4$" of clearance between the bottom of the post and the top of the workpiece.

To get a good performance out of the band saw, it is important that the two thrust bearings support the blade equally. It is best to adjust the height of the post *before* adjusting the thrust bearing and the top guide blocks. You should recheck the top thrust bearing and the top guide blocks for alignment each time you raise or lower the post because the post may not go straight up and down.

Adjusting the Thrust Bearing

The next step is to adjust the thrust bearings. Position the blade weld opposite the bearings. The blade is being used as a straightedge, and the weld is the least straight part of the blade.

For $3/16$" or larger blades, position the two thrust bearings about $1/64$" (0.15") behind the blade. A dollar bill folded twice is a useful way to measure the distance between the back of the blade and the thrust bearing as shown in Illus. 2-5.

When the cut begins, the blade moves rearward and contacts the thrust bearings. When the cutting stops, the blade should move forward again, and the bearings should stop rotating. You can use a feeler gauge or a dollar bill folded twice to determine the correct space between the blade and the bearings. For blades smaller than $3/16$", adjust the thrust bearing so that it moves the blade forward about $1/64$". This means that the blade will always be in contact with the bearing. This gives the smaller blades extra support.

Adjusting the Guide Blocks

Next, adjust the guide blocks. As mentioned, the four guide blocks are held in place by the guide holders that are paired with each thrust bearing above and below the table. Some manufacturers use bearings instead of solid metal guides but the friction between the blade and the metal blocks shortens blade life. In recent years, a nonmetal replacement guide block called Cool Blocks™ has become very popular and now is available from the manufacturers of most band saws.

These nonmetal blocks are a patented fiber with a dry lubricant that greatly decreases the friction between the blade and the blocks. This decreases the heat generated by the blade and thus increases the life of the blade.

Place the metal guide blocks about .004" away from the blade. This is the thickness of a piece of paper, so you can use a dollar bill as a spacer. The distance between the gullet and the front of the guide block should be about $1/64$" because the blade will flex backward during the cut.

Illus. 2-5. The blade should not touch the thrust bearings unless the saw is cutting. There should be a distance of $1/64$" (.015") between the blade and the bearing. A dollar bill folded twice will give you the correct measurement. However, smaller blades such as the $1/16$" and the $1/8$" should touch the bearing.

Another advantage is that the nonmetal blocks can be placed in contact with the blade as shown in Illus. 2-6. This decreases twist and deflection, and improves the accuracy of the band saw cut. The nonmetal blocks are essential for small blades such as the $1/16$" blade, because they can not destroy the very small teeth the way metal blocks can.

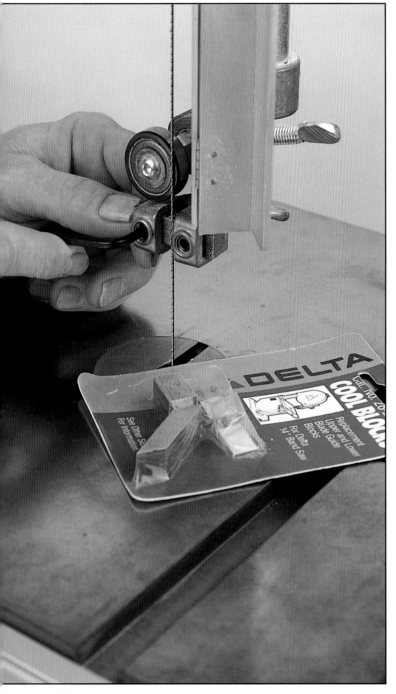

Rounding the Blade Back

Blade performance and blade life is improved by rounding the back of the blade with a stone. A round blade back creates a smooth interaction between the thrust bearing and the blade. There is no sharp blade corner to dig into the thrust bearing. Also, the rounding process smooths the weld. A blade with a round back makes tighter turns easier because the round back has smooth interaction with the saw kerf.

After the guides have been adjusted, hold the stone against the corner of the blade as shown in Illus. 2-7 on opposite page for about a minute. *Wear safety glasses when rounding the blade.* Then do the same thing on the opposite corner.

Next, slowly move the stone to round the back. The more pressure you put on the back, the faster you will remove the metal. Be careful that the inside of the machine is free of sawdust, because sparks could start a fire.

When rounding a $1/8$" or $1/16$" blade, the pressure on the back of the blade may move the blade forward off the front of the wheels. To prevent this, it is best to feed wood into the blade during the rounding process. Pass the wood underneath the elevated stone. This keeps the blade in contact with the thrust bearing as shown in Illus. 2-8 on opposite page.

Illus. 2-6. This band saw is fitted with a $1/16$" blade and Cool Blocks. Cool Blocks are replacement guide blocks that allow the use of small blades and prolong normal blade life. You can extend the life of narrow blades if you follow a few simple rules. When using a narrow blade such as a $1/8$" or $1/16$" blade, keep the top guide about 1" above the workpiece. This will allow the blade to flex rearward slightly during the cut. Cool Blocks should be used because with these blade guides there is less destructive blade heat generated. This is especially important with small blades because there is less metal to act as a heat conductor. The cooler the blade, the longer it will last.

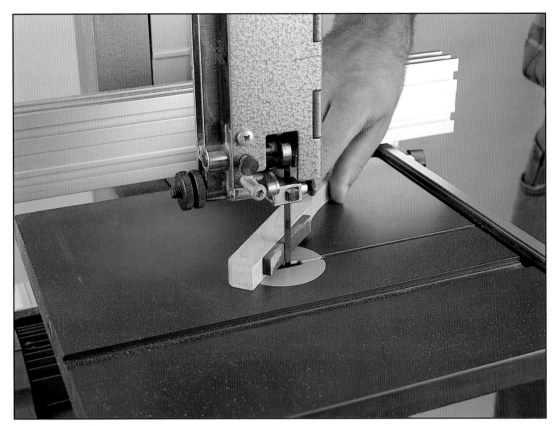

Illus. 2-7.
To round the back of the blade, first stone the corners, then slowly rotate the stone around the back. This process takes about two or three minutes.

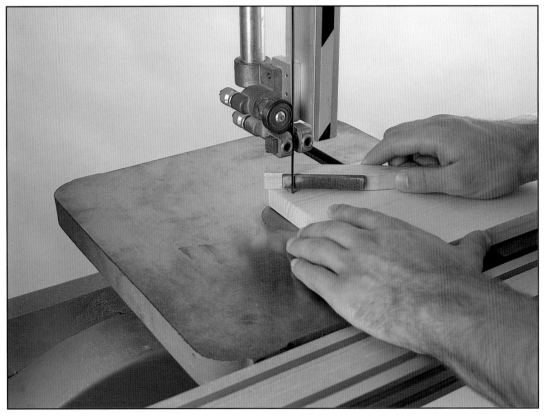

Illus. 2-8.
Feeding wood into a $1/8$"- or $1/16$"-wide blade while rounding it will prevent the stone from pushing the blade forward off the wheels.

Aligning the Band Saw Wheels

If you plan on cutting thick wood, it is recommended that you align your band saw wheels. Aligning band saw wheels is a very simple procedure that should take only a couple of minutes to accomplish. They may or may not be already aligned. The first thing to do is to check for alignment using the following steps.

1. ***Tension the blade.*** Tension the widest blade that you can use on your saw. Tensioning is stretching the blade taut between the wheels. The $^1/_2$" blade is the largest practical size to use on a consumer band saw. Use the tension scale on your band saw.

2. ***Make certain that the wheels are parallel to each other.*** With a straightedge, check to determine if the wheels are parallel with each other. You may have to angle the top wheel to get them parallel. Put the straightedge in the middle of the wheels. If it touches the top and bottom of both wheels, then the wheels are parallel and in line as shown in Illus. 2-9. They are coplanar. If this is the case, you do not have to align them. If the wheels are not in alignment, the straightedge will not touch the top and bottom of both wheel points. Instead, it will either touch the top and bottom of the top wheel or the top and bottom of the lower wheel. In either case, you will have to move one of the wheels to make both wheels coplanar.

3. ***Measure the misalignment.*** It is important to know how far one of the wheels has to be moved to achieve coplanar alignment. This is essential if you are going to achieve coplanar alignment by adding or removing washers from behind the wheel. Measure the misalignment at the top and bottom of the wheel that is not touching the straightedge. The measurements at both points should be the same as shown in Illus. 2-2 on page 14. If they are not exactly the same, angle the top wheel until they are. Once they are the same, that amount (X) is the distance the wheel needs to move to align the wheels. In this situation, move the top wheel forward X amount to achieve alignment.

4. ***Make the adjustment.*** On Sears and Inca models, the adjustment is made with a movable bottom wheel. This is the easiest and most convenient way. The bottom wheel is mounted on a shaft in a keyway (a groove on the shaft that prevents the wheel from spinning on the shaft), and the wheel is locked in place with a setscrew. When making the adjustment, loosen the screw and move the wheel the desired amount. On the Delta and Taiwanese band saws, the adjustment is made on the top wheel, which is mounted on a threaded shaft and held secure with a nut. To make the adjustment, unscrew the nut and then remove the wheels; this will expose the washers. Make the alignment by either adding or removing washers. You can buy additional washers at hardware dealers. After the first alignment, always rotate the wheels several times to make certain the blade is tracking; then recheck the alignment.

Illus. 2-9. The wheels are coplanar if the straightedge touches the tops and bottoms of both wheels. Tension the widest blade that you will use. Here, a $^1/_2$"-wide blade is being tensioned on a Delta band saw.

band saw blades

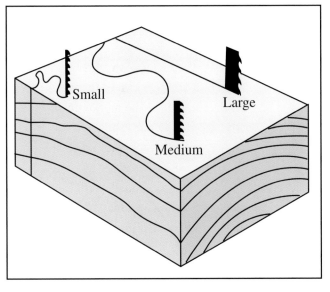

Illus. 3-1. A small blade can cut tighter curves than a large blade. Shown are the tightest curve that can be cut with each size blade.

The difference between a mediocre or an accomplished woodworker often depends on how well one masters the subtleties and small details of the craft. This is especially true when it comes to fine-tuning machinery. One of the most important features of any band saw is the blade you choose. Believe it or not, there are more than 500 different band saw blades on the market, in various sizes, blade body types, and tooth configurations. The blade is a crucial factor in determining the performance of the machine, and ultimately, the quality of the work you produce.

The width of the blade is the most important factor in determining how tight a turn you can cut as shown in Illus. 3-1 and Illus. 3-2.

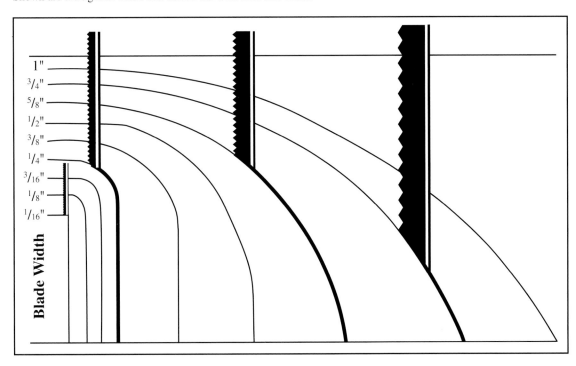

1"
³/₄"
⁵/₈"
¹/₂"
³/₈"
¹/₄"
³/₁₆"
¹/₈"
¹/₁₆"

Blade Width

Illus. 3-2. Radius charts can be found in woodworking books, magazines, and on the boxes in which the blades are purchased.

In this chapter, various types and sizes of band saw blades will be discussed, so you can decipher the manufacturers' specifications when buying a band saw blade. I will also elaborate on which blades I have found to be best for particular woods and woodworking tasks.

A band saw blade is a strip of strong, thin steel, with teeth on one edge that has been welded into a loop. Blade material typically comes in a continuous roll, and then blade manufacturers or saw shops weld up individual blades in different lengths to fit various band saws. A band saw blade must perform two tasks—which are somewhat contradictory. It must flex around the wheels of the saw, yet cut perfectly straight. To accomplish this, the blade body is made from pliable steel that is resistant to metal fatigue.

Blades are distinguished according to several features, including their width and the size and form of their teeth as shown in Illus. 3-3, which determine if the blade will be better suited to coarse or fine cuts, large or small radius curves, thick or thin stock, and hard or soft woods.

Understanding the functions of the various blade features, as well as the nomenclature by which blade sellers describe them, will help you select the best blade for a particular woodcutting job.

Blade Width

Blade width is measured from the flat side of the blade to the tip of its teeth. Consumer-grade band saws typically use blades that range in width from $1/16"$ to $1/2"$. The width determines how tight a radius the blade can cut—the narrower the blade, the tighter the turn. However, the narrower the blade, the more susceptible it is to deflection. For this reason, wider blades are preferred when making straight cuts in thick stock or when resawing.

In most cases, it is best to select the widest blade that will cut the smallest radius curve you need. You can find charts in machinery reference books or sometimes on a blade box that shows blade width/minimum radius. I find it easier to remember a few household items that indicate minimum cutting diameters: a $1/8"$ blade cuts to the diameter of a pencil eraser; a $3/16"$ blade cuts to the

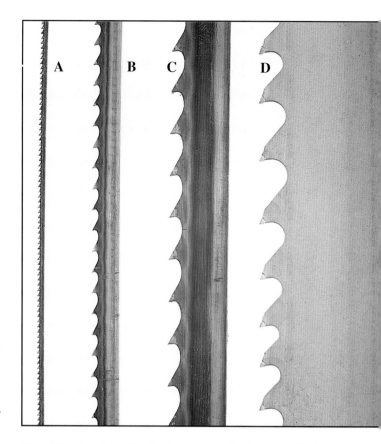

Illus. 3-3. A variety of tooth pitches are available for each blade width. Blades marked A and B have regular teeth. Blade C has hook teeth. Blade D is a carbide-tipped variable pitch. Blades with a variable pitch are used to cut metal pipes and I beams. These types of blades are less prone to vibration. Woodworkers have recently started to use these blades with good results.

diameter of a dime; a $1/4"$ blade cuts to the diameter of a quarter; a $3/8"$ blade cuts to the diameter of the base of a traditional-style teacup; and a $1/2"$ blade cuts to the diameter of the rim of the teacup.

Unless your band saw's wheels are 18" or larger in diameter, a $1/2"$ blade is the widest I recommend for 14" saws. Some owner's manuals say that you can use a $3/4"$ blade—the band saw's crowned wheels only contact wide blades in the center and this can cause the blade to rock back and forth, resulting in excessive vibration. Also, $3/4"$ blades are thicker than narrower blades and tend to break prematurely when they are forced to bend around smaller wheels; it is also difficult for a smaller saw to put enough tension on a wide blade to make it perform properly.

Tooth Pitch

A blade's pitch refers to the size of the teeth, which largely determines both how fast and how smooth the blade will cut. Pitch is usually stated as teeth per inch (t.p.i.), which is the number of teeth on 1" of the blade. Generally, the finer the pitch (the more teeth per inch), the slower, but smoother the cut. The coarser the pitch (the less teeth per inch), the faster, but rougher the cut. Narrow blades usually have fine pitch. There are some wide blades available with 14 t.p.i. or 18 t.p.i. and these usually provide the best combination of fine teeth, blade strength, and heat dispersion for cutting nonferrous metals and very hard exotic woods. It is important to match the blade pitch to the hardness of the material as shown in Illus. 3-4.

To keep a band saw blade from binding in the kerf of the cut, the teeth are "set"—bent slightly to alternating sides to make the front of the blade thicker than the back. The number of set teeth on any given blade is usually determined by the pitch. On blades with a fine pitch, every third is a "raker" or unset tooth. The tooth before each raker is set to one side and the tooth after each raker is set to the other side. On some coarse-pitch blades, every fifth or seventh tooth is a raker and those between are set alternatively.

When selecting blade pitch, you should consider how thick your workpieces will be and pick a blade that will have at least three teeth in the workpiece at all times during the cut. This guarantees a smooth transition—as the tooth at the top enters the wood, the bottom tooth exits. By choosing the proper pitch, you will get a clean cut, little vibration, easy feeding, and long blade life.

The harder the wood, the finer the pitch should be; the softer the wood, the coarser the pitch. If the pitch is too coarse, you will notice vibration and chatter. If it is too fine, the blade will produce excessive heat, which shortens blade life. A fine-pitch blade also requires more feed pressure, which produces more heat.

The moisture and resin content of the wood must also be considered. Green or wet wood requires a coarser pitch, no finer than 6 t.p.i. to keep the blade gullets (the hollows between the teeth) from clogging with chips. This is especially true with thick stock. Resinous woods like pine (even when properly dried) also require a coarser pitch, no finer than 8 t.p.i. so they will not gum up the blade. Wood resins can even bake onto the teeth of a hot blade, requiring cleaning with mineral spirits and a fine wire brush. Nonresinous woods such as oak, maple, and walnut can be cut with

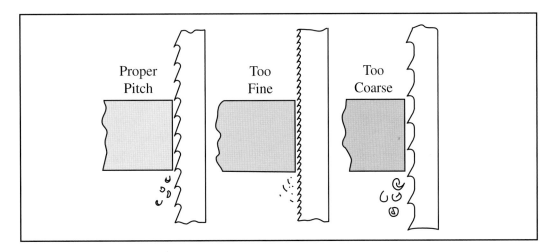

Illus. 3-4. Pitch is measured in teeth per inch (t.p.i.). It is common for wide blades to have fewer teeth per inch than narrow blades which often have many teeth. If a blade has a pitch that is too coarse, the teeth will dull prematurely. Hard material requires a finer pitch than soft material. If you want to make the most efficient cut, make certain to use a blade with the proper pitch.

a fine-pitch blade (14, 18, or 24 t.p.i.) without clogging or gumming problems. Very dense exotics like rosewood, ebony, and teak require a blade with between 12 and 18 t.p.i. These woods are hard enough to quickly destroy a narrow blade due to the heat generated from cutting. Therefore, use a wide blade with these exotics if possible. A wide blade body acts as a heat sink, keeping the teeth cooler and increasing the length of time they stay sharp.

Tooth Form

The term "tooth form" describes the shape of the tooth, the size and shape of the gullet between the teeth, and the rake. The rake is the angle of the cutting edge of the tooth relative to an imaginary line perpendicular to the back edge of the blade. The rake determines the angle at which the tooth contacts the wood and is the single most important factor affecting a blade's cutting performance.

Woodcutting band saw blades usually come in three tooth types: standard, skip, and hook. The standard and skip designs have a 0° rake. In contrast, a hook tooth blade has a positive rake of 5°, 7°, or 10°, causing the teeth to cut more aggressively as shown in Illus. 3-5. The hook tooth blade produces a rougher cut than a standard or skip tooth blade. Standard or skip tooth blades work with a scraping action, causing a smoother cut, while at the same time generating more heat.

A standard tooth blade has a gullet the same size as the tooth. These blades are most commonly available in narrow widths such as 1/16" and 1/8", and the latter is only available with standard teeth. Because of their numerous teeth and 0° rake, these blades produce very smooth cuts.

A skip tooth blade, as its name implies, has half as many teeth as the standard tooth, and thus larger gullets between teeth. The skip tooth design comes in all blade widths except 1/16", which is not wide enough to accommodate the large gullets. Skip tooth blades cut much faster than standard blades, but the finish they leave behind is coarser—especially on crosscuts. They also last longer because they generate less heat as fewer teeth means less friction. In addition, skip tooth blades have larger gullets than regular blades, which make them less prone to breakage and their larger capacity makes for good resawing. However, skip tooth blades tend to vibrate (called harmonic flutter), which can leave a rough diagonal corduroy pattern on the surface of the cut. If you encounter this condition, reduce your feed rate, change your blade tension (either increasing or decreasing it slightly), or switch to a finer tooth blade.

The positive rake angle on a hook tooth blade makes its teeth bite into the workpiece more aggressively. This design, combined with rounded gullets that resist clogging, give hook tooth blades several significant advantages when they are used for cutting wood with the grain, such as ripping or resawing. The positive rake teeth actually pull themselves into the stock so cutting requires less feed pressure. This places less stress on the blade body, decreasing the likelihood of deflection and wandering cuts, and less pressure on the band saw's thrust bearings. Because of these char-

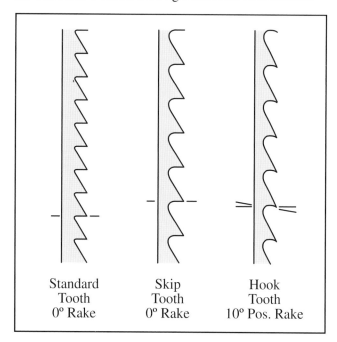

Illus. 3-5. Standard and skip teeth have a 0° rake angle. Hook teeth have a positive angle which is usually 10°.

acteristics, hook tooth blades stay sharp longer and produce good results at a moderate blade tension. However, hook tooth blades require more horsepower while cutting and they tend to make rough crosscuts.

Choosing the Right Blade

Beyond specifying a blade that is the correct length for your band saw, selecting the right combination of the features described can make choosing a blade complex and confusing. Illus. 3-6 shows the common terminology used to describe various parts of the blade. Unfortunately, there is not a single magic blade that does everything well. However, you can easily assemble a small collection of blades that will let you do almost any band-sawing task cleanly and efficiently.

For almost all my work building furniture and cabinets, I use one of five different blades and switch to a special-purpose blade only when necessary. My two narrowest are a $1/16$" 24 t.p.i. blade and a $1/8$" 14 t.p.i. blade. The $1/16$" blade yields an exceptionally smooth cut and I find it much faster for sawing intricate patterns or open fretwork than a scroll. The blade's only weakness is that its teeth are too fine for resinous woods such as pine and cherry. The $1/8$" blade

also yields a fairly smooth cut, and saws through pine with less clogging. It is my blade of choice for cross-cutting small pieces and sawing fine joinery such as dovetails. This size is also a good choice for fine cuts in harder woods like maple, hickory, and exotics. I prefer the standard tooth design, but a $1/8$" skip tooth blade is also available for faster yet rougher cuts, such as for sawing out a curvaceous cabriole leg.

Among medium-width blades, my choices are a $1/4$" 4 t.p.i. skip tooth and a $1/4$" 6 t.p.i. hook tooth. These two blades provide a wide range of cutting options and either blade can be left on the band saw as a general-purpose blade. The 6 t.p.i. is better for a finer finish cut in harder wood, while the 4 t.p.i. skip tooth is better in thicker stock for quickly cutting out curved parts. The 4 t.p.i. can even be used for resawing in a pinch, and it is also my choice for cutting basic joinery such as tenons. If you plan to cut very hard woods, you might also want to keep a $1/4$" 8 t.p.i. standard or skip tooth blade on hand.

My favorite blade for making long, straight cuts and for resawing is a $1/2$" 3 t.p.i. hook tooth. If you are cutting a lot of medium-thick ($1 1/4$" to $1 1/2$") stock or dense exotics, you may consider selecting a 4 t.p.i. or 5 t.p.i. hook tooth blade instead. For your most demanding resawing jobs such as cutting a board into thin veneer, use a new blade or set aside a sharp $1/2$" blade just for resawing.

There are hundreds of special-purpose band saw blades designed for cutting metal, plastic, and other materials. For particleboard, wood with lots of knots, or very hard exotics, a bimetal blade, with its durable high-speed steel teeth, is a good choice. However, I find that these blades are impractical for general woodworking. Besides being expensive, bimetal blades are primarily designed to run at low speeds in metal-cutting applications, and the stiff blade body tends to vibrate or fatigue prematurely on saws with wheels less than 20" in diameter.

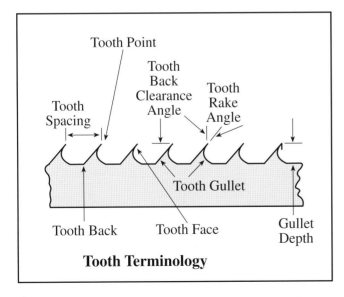

Tooth Terminology

Illus. 3-6. A clarification of the terms used to describe band saw blades. The tooth angle is the angle of the point created by the intersection of the tooth face and the tooth back.

curved cuts

One advantage the band saw has over other power tools is that it can cut curves in both thick and thin wood. A curved cut is possible because the workpiece can be rotated around the narrow blade. When the workpiece is turned sharply, the back of the blade rubs against the saw kerf. This is the smallest turn that is possible to make. If you rotate the workpiece past this point, the blade body will start to twist. To prevent the blade from twisting, make certain you feed the workpiece forward into the blade during a sharp turn, and that you use a blade of the appropriate width.

It is important that you plan ahead when making turns. Planning helps to minimize wasted material and decrease the difficulty of the cut. For example, when making a piece that has parallel curves, it is possible to make one curved cut and then glue the two separate pieces back together with their flat sides in contact with each other. This saves time and material and increases the accuracy of the cut. If you choose the grain carefully, the glue line will be nearly impossible to see.

When cutting multiple pieces with parallel curves, it is possible to use the rip fence to space the width of the workpiece. A rip fence is an accessory used to control the saw when a cut is being made along the grain of the wood. The workpiece should be touching the rip fence about $1/4"$ in front of the saw blade as shown in Illus. 4-1. This technique allows you to make multiple pieces that are exactly the same size with very little effort. It works on small and large workpieces as shown in Illus. 4-2.

Illus. 4-1. When making a curved cut, slowly rotate the workpiece. As the cut progresses, slowly move your hands to the back of the workpiece. Use your thumb to move the piece forward. The curved side of the workpiece is against the rip fence about $1/4"$ in front of the blade.

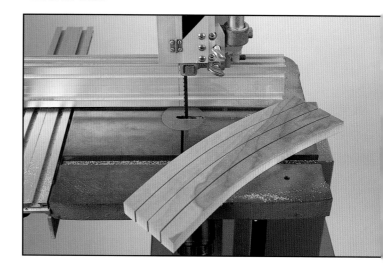

Illus. 4-2. It is easy to cut multiple pieces with parallel curves if you use the rip fence to space the width of the workpiece. The distance between the blade and the rip fence determines the width of the workpiece. Keep the workpiece against the rip fence while making the cut.

Single-point Technique for Curves

As previously discussed, the rip fence can be used as a rotation point for determining the width of the workpiece. This technique works well if the piece has a gentle curve in one direction. If the piece curves in several directions, a similar technique is used, except that the rotation point is a pointed guide rather than a rip fence. Clamp or bolt the pointed guide to the rip fence or the table as shown in Illus. 4-3.

If the curve to be cut is a gentle curve, use a stick with a rounded point. Hold the edge of the workpiece against the point. You have to "fishtail" or angle the piece into the blade at the correct angle as shown in Illus. 4-4.

This technique requires some skill and concentration. It is particularly useful on pieces with multiple curves, such as chair backs as shown in Illus. 4-5. It is also useful on small objects with multiple curves, such as band-sawn boxes. When the single-point technique is used for small objects or tight curves, the point on the guide should be sharp rather than rounded.

Do not force the work or bend or twist the blade. Feed the work gently into the blade. Remember that you must be feeding the wood forward when you are making a turn—especially a tight turn. A gentle, smooth rhythm will generate the best results.

Illus. 4-4. Start the cut with the corner against the point of the stick. Continue the cut by putting light pressure against the point. It is not enough to just hold the piece against the point and push. You must move the workpiece back and forth (called fishtailing).

Illus. 4-3. It is useful to make a single-point guide to help you with a variety of cutting situations.

Illus. 4-5. Multiple pieces cut from the same board.

When sawing, you usually follow a line on the workpiece. A pencil line works best because it does not leave a permanent stain and it can be erased. Saw near the outside of the line, but not actually on it. This way, the line will still be intact if you decide to sand or plane the edge and you will still be able to see the desired shape.

Use both hands to feed the wood into the blade. Keep them on opposite sides of the workpiece. Never cross your hands. If you are in an awkward position, keep one hand on the workpiece and move the other hand. Always keep your fingers away from the pencil line—especially at the end of the cut.

Use a jig or clamp to hold odd-shaped or small pieces during the sawing process. Small pieces are more dangerous to cut than large pieces because your fingers are closer to the blade.

Think ahead and plan your saw cuts. Although the band saw is easy to use, proper technique usage is required to use the saw efficiently.

If you must back out, turn the saw off first. You can also tilt the top wheel backward slightly to decrease the likelihood of the saw blade coming forward off the wheels when you back out.

Intarsia

Two different pieces are often used next to each other as a decorative element. When veneer is used, the technique is referred to as "marquetry." When solid wood is used, the technique is referred to as "intarsia."

To use the techniques of marquetry or intarsia, you usually have to cut the two mating pieces simultaneously. When the cuts are long or gentle curves, the two pieces will fit exceptionally well if the blade and table are at 90° to each other.

If the curves are tight or the design is small, the fit between the matching pieces requires that the table be slightly angled. The angle accurately helps to compensate for the wood lost to the saw kerf. You will have to experiment with scrap wood to get the appropriate angle. The angle will depend on the saw width and the wood thickness.

Recently, the Wisconsin Woodworkers Guild published a chart after one of its members did a demonstration of intarsia. The top piece of wood mates with the bottom piece after the angled saw cut is made. This Intarsia Chart was created by engineer Beau Lowerr. Using this chart, it is easy to determine the right degree of table tilt that is necessary to create a tight fit.

INTARSIA CHART

"BACKGROUND" WOOD THICKNESS

DEGREES TABLE TILT FROM HORIZONTAL

		0.125	0.250	0.375	0.500	0.750
S	0.015	6.9	3.4			
A	0.016	7.4	3.7			
W	0.017	7.8	3.9			
	0.018	8.3	4.1			
K	0.019	8.7	4.4	2.9		
E	0.020		4.6	3.1		
R	0.021		4.8	3.2		
F	0.022		5.0	3.4		
	0.023		5.3	3.5		
	0.024		5.5	3.7		
	0.025		5.7	3.8	2.9	1.9
	0.026			4.0	3.0	2.0
	0.027			4.1	3.1	2.1
	0.028			4.3	3.2	2.1
	0.029			4.4	3.3	2.2
	0.030			4.6	3.4	2.3

Scroll Sawing

In the past, a special piece of equipment called a scroll saw with narrow blades was used to make tight turns. This procedure is called scroll sawing.

Until recently, the narrowest blade that was available for the band saw was $1/8$" wide. The latest development for band saws is a blade that is only $1/16$" wide as shown in Illus. 4-6.

With the introduction of Cool Blocks (nonmetallic guide blocks) and $1/16$" blades, it is possible to do scroll saw work with a band saw. This blade makes extremely tight turns, similar to those made by an expensive scroll saw blade. In fact, in some instances, it is very hard to tell the difference between work done with a band saw and that done with an expensive scroll saw.

A $1/16$" band saw blade has a very fine pitch (several teeth per inch), which allows the final cut to be smooth. It can also make very accurate straight cuts that would be extremely hard, if not impossible, to do with a scroll saw.

Narrow band saw blades can also be used to make cuts in thick material. This is why the $1/16$" blade is becoming very popular, even with those who already have a scroll saw.

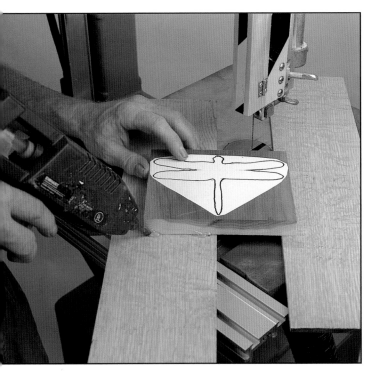

To use the smaller blades successfully, you will have to make some changes in the standard adjustment procedure. It is necessary to replace the metal guides. Cool Blocks seem to work best. Place these blocks just behind the gullets.

As mentioned in Chapter 3, you should round the back of a small band saw blade. When using $1/8$" or $1/16$" blades, the pressure on the back of the blade may bring the blade forward off the front of the wheels. To prevent this, it is best to feed wood into the blade during the rounding process. Pass the wood underneath the elevated stone. This keeps the blade in contact with the thrust bearing.

A $1/8$" and $1/16$" blade will last significantly longer when the guide is raised. However, this exposes about an inch of blade, which could be a potential hazard, so use extra caution.

Inside Cuts Using a Narrow Blade

You can use a narrow blade on a band saw to make inside cuts. To do this, cut two halves of the piece and then glue them together. We will refer to this technique as the "cut and glue" technique.

A paper pattern is attached with rubber cement to the top of a walnut board. The walnut board and the pattern are attached to one lighter $1/4$" oak board with a daub of hot-melt glue. The table is tilted 7° and the cut on the pattern line is started and then stopped after the blade is finished cutting both boards. The two oak boards are held together temporarily with a drop of hot-melt glue.

Illus. 4-6. This band saw is fitted with a $1/16$" blade and Cool Blocks. Cool Blocks are replacement guide blocks that allow the use of small blades and prolong normal blade life. The blade and the front of the blocks are aligned with each other. Use rubber cement to attach the pattern to the top piece. The top piece is temporarily attached to the bottom piece with hot-melt glue.

The cut is continued as shown in Illus. 4-7. The pattern is cut out as shown in Illus. 4-8. To remove the wood from the saw, the hot-melt glue drops that hold the lighter oak pieces together are removed. The oak boards are glued together and the dragonfly fits extremely well in the opening as shown in Illus. 4-9.

Illus. 4-9. Two pieces will fit tightly together if you cut tight curves and tilt the table at the correct angle.

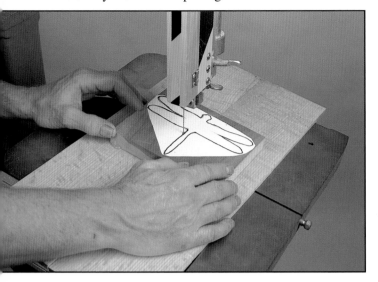

Illus. 4-7. After you have cut into both pieces, use tape or hot-melt glue to hold the bottom pieces together. Here a $^1/_{16}$"-wide blade is being used with the table tilted.

Making the Cabriole Leg

One task that is often intimidating for beginners is the making of a cabriole leg. This job is actually quite simple if the correct sequence is followed. Laying out the pattern correctly is critical as shown in Illus. 4-10 on opposite page. Since one often makes sets of four, it may get confusing. The knees and feet should be pointing toward each other. It is much easier to make joints with a square board, so do the mortising, etc., before making the curved cuts.

Cut the straight lines first using the rip fence as shown in Illus. 4-11 on opposite page. Next, cut the backs of the legs as shown in Illus. 4-12 on opposite page. Then make the long cuts. It is best to have enough stock so you do not cut through the pattern on the outside of the leg. When finishing the cut, stop about $^1/_{16}$" from the end as shown in Illus. 4-12 on opposite page. This technique is called the "hinge" cut. If it is done correctly, the wood will open, making it easy for you to back the blade out of the cut. Using the

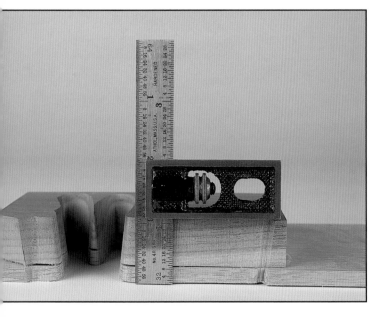

Illus. 4-8. When the inside piece is removed, you can see the angled wall created by the tilt of the table at the correct angle.

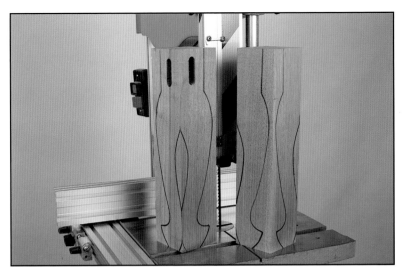

Illus. 4-10. When making legs, do the joinery such as mortising first. When you are making a cabriole leg, use the same pattern on two adjacent sides. The cabriole leg patterns point away from each other at the back of the leg shown on the left side of the photograph. The patterns shown on the front part of the leg point toward each other as shown on the right.

Illus. 4-11. Make the straight entry cut by using the rip fence.

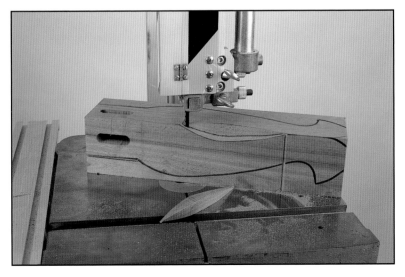

Illus. 4-12. Cut the back of the leg, but do not complete the cut. Leave about $^1/_{16}$" of material between the cut and the straight release cut. The "hinge cut" allows you to open the kerf, which makes it easier for you to back the blade out. This allows the adjacent pattern to remain intact. Try to leave a flat area between the heels and the back of the leg. This can be rounded later.

31

rip fence will guarantee that the crosscut for the bottom of the leg will be adjacent to each other as shown in Illus. 4-13. Cut out the small pieces of waste, keeping the long cuts for last as shown in Illus. 4-14. If you accidentally go too far, you can tape the piece back on. It is important to have the long piece positioned well because it has the pattern for the next cut on the adjacent side as shown in Illus. 4-15 and Illus. 4-16.

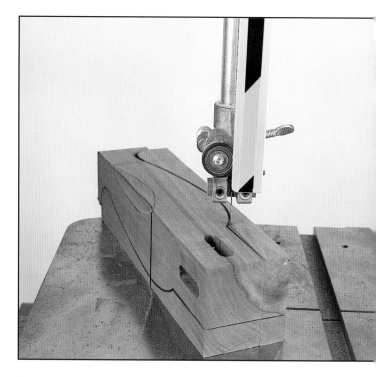

Illus. 4-15. Use a hinge cut on the cuts so you do not remove the pattern from the adjacent side.

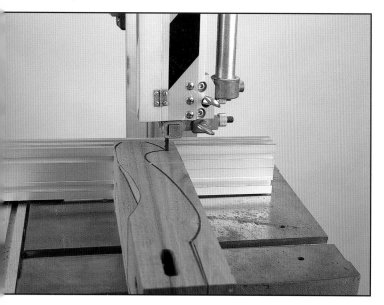

Illus. 4-13. Use the rip fence for guiding the crosscut—this guarantees that the adjacent cuts will line up with each other.

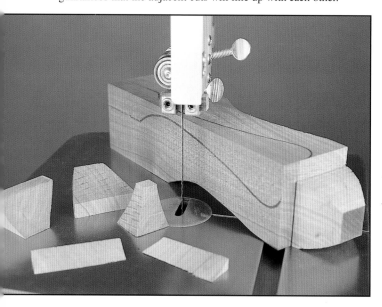

Illus. 4-14. Cut the waste pieces from the bottom of the leg.

Illus. 4-16. Cut the waste pieces from the sides of the leg by finishing the hinge cuts.

Rotate the workpiece so you can expose the pattern and finish the cut. Break the hinge cut. This will expose the completed leg as shown in Illus. 4-17. A completed leg with a pile of waste is shown in Illus. 4-18.

Sanding the leg takes a minimal amount of time if you use an inflatable drum sander. You can adjust the drum sander with air pressure so that it fits the shape of the leg.

Illus. 4-17. Cut the waste pieces from the adjacent sides of the leg.

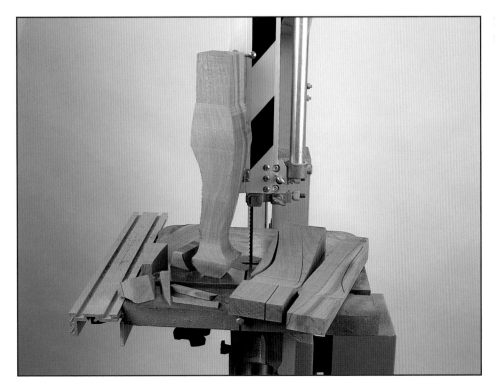

Illus. 4-18. Completed leg with its pile of scrap.

straight cuts

Although the band saw is usually associated with making curves, a variety of straight cuts are easily made with the saw. In fact, it is often used to rip small pieces of wood because it is much safer than either a radial arm saw or a table saw.

The band saw can also cut thicker stock than the radial arm or table saw and is therefore often used to make straight cuts in thick material. The one disadvantage of cutting with the band saw is that the saw cut is not as smooth as those made by the table or radial arm saw. However, most of the time the band-sawn edge can be either planed or jointed straight and smooth.

There are two methods for making straight band saw cuts. One is to feed the work into the blade freehand. The other is to use a jig or fixture to control the workpiece. To maintain consistency and accuracy, you should use a jig or fixture whenever possible.

The fixtures most often used are the miter slot, the rip fence, and the tap jig. In special situations, a fixture that slides into the miter slot is used.

Crosscutting

A crosscut is a cut made across the grain of the workpiece. A miter slot is the fixture commonly used when a crosscut is made. The head of the miter slot adjusts to the desired angle of the cut. The rip fence can also be used to crosscut small pieces. If you are going to make a lot of straight crosscuts, it is recommended that you use a narrow blade with standard teeth.

Use a blade with a pitch of 12 to 14 teeth per inch (t.p.i.). This type of blade works best for crosscutting. The $1/8$" blades usually have such a pitch. Because narrow blades flex rearward during the cut, they make very accurate cuts. The $1/16$" blade with 24 t.p.i. will crosscut nonresinous woods very efficiently as shown in Illus. 5-1. Cool Blocks, which are nonmetallic replacement guide blocks, can be used in contact with the blade and increase the accuracy of the cut by decreasing sideways deflection.

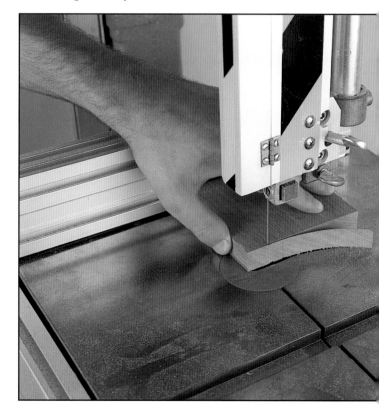

Illus. 5-1. These straight crosscuts can be made with a miter guide or the rip fence. The $1/16$" blade will very accurately crosscut with the use of the rip fence.

Ripping and Resawing

Ripping is a cut made with the grain of the wood. The term "ripping" is used when the board lays flat on the table and the term "resawing" is used when the board is sawn while resting on its edge.

There are three techniques for making straight band saw cuts with a fence. The three techniques for guiding the work are the single-point, the straight rip fence, and the curved rip fence which is a combination of the other two techniques.

The first technique requires that the wood be advanced into the blade while in contact with a single point. The rationale for using the single-point is that the saw may tend to cut at a slight angle. This is often called "lead." The single-point allows the operator to feed the wood into the blade at a slight angle, which compensates for blade lead as shown in Illus. 5-2. Because this technique requires constant attention, it is not recommended for any volume of work. With a little practice, you will get satisfactory results with the single-point method as shown in Illus. 5-3.

The second technique is to use the rip fence as a guide. If you are going to do a lot of cutting, it is best to adjust the angle of the rip fence to correspond with blade lead. This is a fairly simple procedure that will only take a minute.

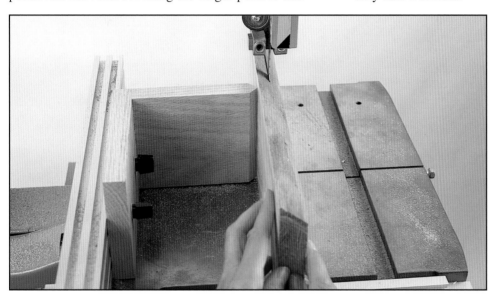

Illus. 5-2. The single-point technique allows the wood to be fed into the blade at a slight angle. This angle compensates for blade lead.

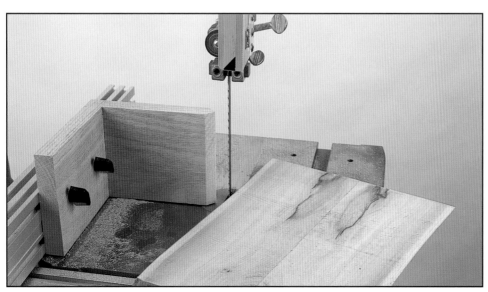

Illus. 5-3. Resawing is cutting a board in half along its width. Resawing exposes the two inside surfaces of the board. The two surfaces are mirror images of each other. When the two matching halves are glued together, it is called bookmatching.

Adjusting the Rip Fence Angle

1. Make a straight pencil mark on the edge of the board.

2. Feed the wood into the blade, cutting next to the pencil mark. If the blade is leading, you will have to angle it slightly to keep it cutting along the pencil mark as shown in Illus. 5-4.

3. Stop the cut in the middle of the board and mark the angle on the table with a pencil. This is the angle at which the blade is leading, thus it is the best angle at which to feed work into the blade.

4. Adjust the angle of the rip fence to correspond with the mark on the table as shown in Illus. 5-5.

5. Complete the cut and observe the piece between the rip fence and the blade. If the rip fence is set at the correct angle it will cut straight and the wood will slide between the rip fence and the board just touching both without binding as shown in Illus. 5-6.

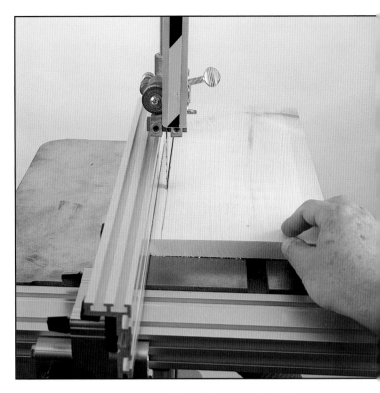

Illus. 5-5. Loosen the rip fence bolts with a wrench and change the angle of the rip fence so it corresponds to the angle of the test cut.

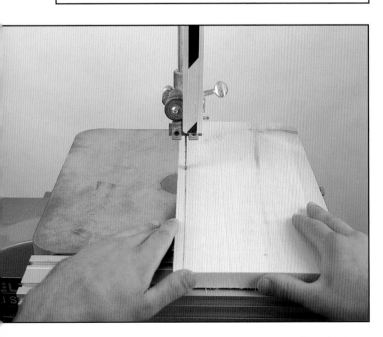

Illus. 5-4. Feed the wood into the blade on the pencil mark. To make a straight cut, you may have to angle the workpiece slightly. This is the angle at which the saw blade cuts best.

Illus. 5-6. If the rip fence is adjusted at the correct angle, the wood will slide between the blade and the rip fence, just touching both, but not binding.

Each time you change the blade, it is a good idea to check, and possibly adjust, the angle of the rip fence.

Once the rip fence angle is adjusted, check to make certain that the table is square and that the rip fence is also square to the table as shown in Illus. 5-7.

Rest the workpiece against the rip fence and advance the wood into the blade holding it with even pressure at a point in front of the blade as shown in Illus. 5-8.

If the rip fence angle is adjusted correctly and you use the proper sawing technique, the result will be a uniform cut as shown in Illus. 5-9.

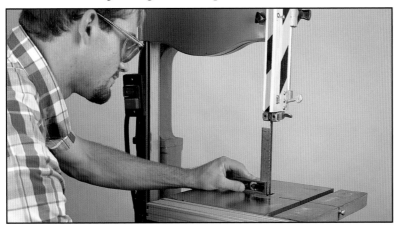

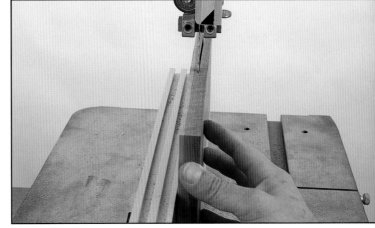

Illus. 5-7. When resawing, double check to make certain the table is square to the blade.

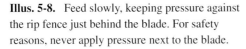

Illus. 5-8. Feed slowly, keeping pressure against the rip fence just behind the blade. For safety reasons, never apply pressure next to the blade.

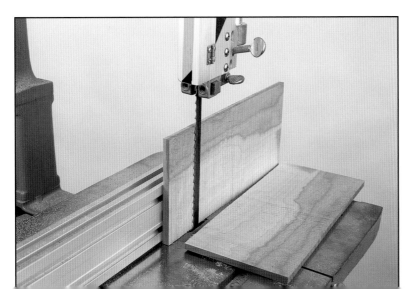

Illus. 5-9. Proper machine alignment, a $1/2''$ 3 t.p.i. blade, and a slow steady feed rate yields a uniform piece of veneer.

The third technique is to use a curved rip fence to guide the work. It can be either a curved wood auxiliary rip fence as shown in Illus. 5-10, or a curved aluminum extrusion attached to the standard rip fence, which is a hybrid of the two previously mentioned techniques. It offers the advantages of the single-point and the rip fence techniques. It provides the stability of a solid rip fence, but it also allows the option of angling the feed direction to adjust for blade lead.

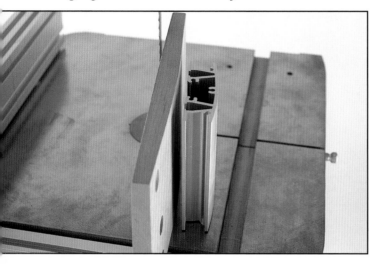

Illus. 5-10. The 5"-high curved wood rip fence is about $1/4$" thicker in the middle than on the two ends.

Illus. 5-11. A commercially available curved aluminum rip fence has about $1/8$" curve in about $3^1/2$".

The curved wood rip fence is designed to be about a foot long and to be roughly $1/4$" thicker in the middle than on the two ends. It is attached to the rip fence with screws or bolts. The commercially available curved aluminum rip fence is about $3^1/2$" wide and curves about $1/8$" toward the edge as shown in Illus. 5-11. It is designed to bolt or clamp to the standard rip fence on the saw as shown in Illus. 5-12. The middle of the curved aluminum rip fence is positioned about $1/4$" in front of the blade as shown in Illus. 5-13.

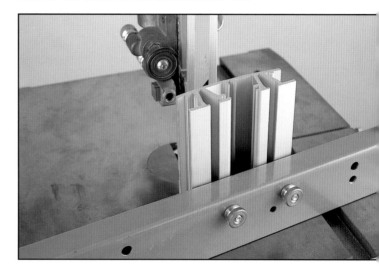

Illus. 5-12. The curved aluminum rip fence can either be bolted or clamped to a standard rip fence. Holes were drilled in this Delta rip fence and it is attached with bolts which fit in the "T" slots.

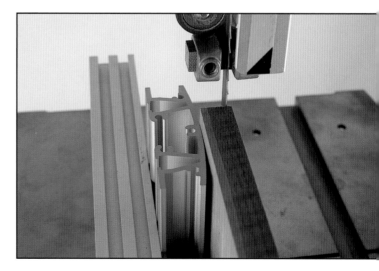

Illus. 5-13. The top of the curve should be about $1/4$" in front of the blade.

The workpiece rests against the apex of the curve before the cut is started.

As the cut progresses, a slight change in angle is easily accomplished by moving the board laterally as shown in Illus. 5-14.

With little practice it is easy to achieve professional quality resawing as shown in Illus. 5-15.

The huge advantage of the curved rip fence is that it is easy to do and it works with every blade. This avoids the annoyance of having to check and adjust the angle of the rip fence each time that you change a blade. It is much easier to use than the single-point rip fence because it supports the board much better and allows for very slight angle adjustments.

Illus. 5-14. Feed slowly, keeping pressure against the curved rip fence in front of the blade. For safety reasons, never apply pressure next to the blade.

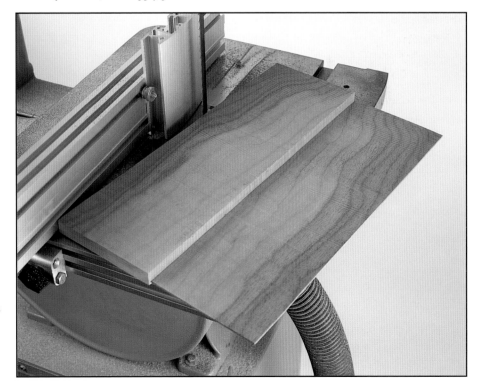

Illus. 5-15. Proper machine alignment, a sharp blade, and a slow steady feed rate yields a uniform piece of veneer. The curved rip fence is the easiest way to resaw.

Resawing and Bookmatching

Resawing is the process of cutting a board in half along its width as shown in Illus. 5-16 and Illus. 5-17.

The ability to cut thick stock, such as resawing for making veneers, bookmatching, or cutting flitches from small logs, has broad appeal to the experimental woodworker because it greatly enhances ones design ability without requiring extra tools or accessories. When the board is resawn and the two pieces are lying flat next to each other, you will note that they are mirror images of each other. When these two boards are glued together, it is called "bookmatching."

Bookmatching greatly enhances the character of a piece and is useful on all flat surfaces such as tabletops and doors.

Illus. 5-16. Resawing a quarter-sawn piece of wood will produce nearly identical grain designs. This arrangement shows the two sides from the inside of the tree touching. The lighter sapwood is on the outside. Inset: This is the opposite of the photograph in Illus. 5-16. The lighter sapwood is on the inside.

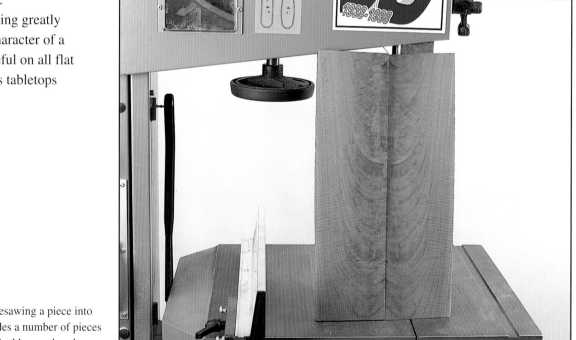

Illus. 5-17. Resawing a piece into veneers provides a number of pieces of a rare or valuable wood such as this piece of crotch walnut.

Selecting the Blade

Cutting thick stock puts maximum strain on both the blade and the machine. The blade used should be the largest blade that your saw can handle. For a band saw with wheels 14" or smaller, the largest recommended blade is a $1/2$" three t.p.i. hook. This blade width offers maximum beam strength, which has the ability to resist deflection. The hook tooth cuts aggressively and the large gullet has the capacity to carry the waste through the stock. The blade must be sharp, so always begin with a new or resharpened blade. As the blade dulls, the cutting speed will slow and the tendency to wander or lead will increase.

Tensioning the Blade

One of the most arguable aspects of the band saw is the amount of tension to be used. If your saw is well adjusted, and you have a sharp blade, you should be able to slice off veneers with the tension scale at the $1/2$" or $3/4$" setting. You may want to increase the tension slightly as the blade dulls. However, increasing tension is not a magical solution. It can actually aggravate problems by pulling or twisting the frame out of proper alignment. Bearings and shafts wear rapidly if the saw is overtensioned.

Guiding the Workpiece

Check to ensure that the table is square to the blade and that the rip fence is square to the table. If the blade and the rip fence are both square to the table, they should be parallel. The feed rate is very important. A slow and steady feed rate is best. It is imperative that the blade not deflect or twist because once the blade starts on a wayward path, it is extremely difficult to get it straight again. Keep pressure against the rip fence just behind the blade. For safety reasons, avoid applying hand pressure near the blade. The blade could deflect and cut through the side of the workpiece.

Good resawing is the result of a combination of factors. Proper machine alignment, good blade choice, and a slow steady feed rate yields a uniform workpiece.

Sawing by Eye

It is possible to make straight cuts without line guides. This technique is called "sawing by eye" and is shown in Illus. 5-18 and Illus. 5-19.

The cut is started and effort is made to keep the kerf visible on each side of the blade. As the cut progresses, the kerf usually expands making it easier to see. This is a particularly useful technique for rough wood.

Illus. 5-18. When sawing by eye, feed the wood straight into the blade. Try to sight down the side of the blade and keep the kerf of the cut visible.

Illus. 5-19. As the cut progresses, the kerf opens and it is easier to see.

After the piece is cut, it should be jointed flat and squared if it is a corner. Pieces of wood that are cut up for firewood are often beautiful and useful if processed correctly. If a short piece of wood is cut into narrow widths, the wood dries quickly.

Because this piece of oak is close to being quarter-sawn, it will dry and remain straight. The three pieces cut from the side of the chunk of firewood have a very similar grain pattern as shown in Illus. 5-20.

My 20" band saw is fitted with a variable pitch 1"-wide blade as shown in Illus. 5-21. This blade will make an extremely clean cut in a variety of wet or dry woods. It is a wonderful experience to be able to slice off pieces of wood 12" wide.

Illus. 5-20. This shows the piece of wood from the earlier photographs after it was jointed and then sawn into $3/16$" pieces. Because it is from a quartered piece, the grain on each piece is very similar.

Illus. 5-21. This is the wood and the blade from the previous photographs. This is a 1"-wide variable pitch blade. The teeth get progressively larger and then smaller. Notice the quality of the cut.

patterns and templates

The usual practice when using the band saw is to cut next to a pencil line which is the representation of the shape you are trying to cut. A pattern is the shape of the desired item that you plan to cut. It can be drawn directly onto the workpiece, or it can be drawn or copied onto a piece of paper, which is then attached to the workpiece. The paper can be taped in place or it can be attached with an adhesive such as rubber cement as shown in Illus. 6-1.

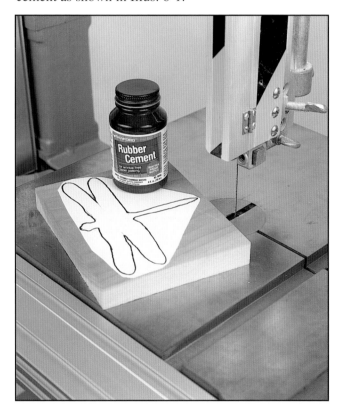

Illus. 6-1. Rubber cement is a good way to attach a paper pattern to a piece of wood. The rubber cement easily peels off the workpiece.

Patterns

Patterns are often found in books or magazines. They can also be ordered from a variety of sources. You may use the exact pattern or you may want to change it slightly. Usually when you build something from scratch, it does not turn out the way that you would like it to. The advantage of using a pattern is that you know exactly what the project will look like. There are a number of ways to make patterns. If you have good drawing skills, you can draw the pattern to scale and then revise the drawing as it suits you.

If you decide to use a pattern from a book or a magazine, you will have to transfer the shape to your workpiece. Usually the pattern is printed in a smaller version to save space. When the grid is enlarged to the point so that each cube is 1" square, the pattern is the correct size.

To enlarge the pattern, you can either make a grid on a piece of paper or use a sheet of graph paper which already has grids. Using the intersecting lines as a reference, transfer the pattern using corresponding dots. It may be helpful to number the lines in both directions on both the large and small patterns. Use a French curve, profile gauge, or curved rulers to connect the dots forming the lines of the desired pattern.

Types of Patterns

• Full Pattern

The full pattern is used when the shape of the object is not symmetrical (its proportions are not balanced). It is important to consider the direction of the wood's grain when laying out a pattern on the piece of wood. The wood's grain runs the length of the pattern.

43

• Half Pattern

When the object is symmetrical, a half pattern is the best pattern to use. A half pattern is only half of the shape. You can use the same pattern for both sides of the object by drawing one side and then flipping the pattern over.

• Quarter Pattern

When the object has four corners that are the same, such as an ellipse, a quarter pattern is useful. The pattern is flipped left to right, and then top to bottom.

• Double Pattern

When the object has the same profile from two adjacent sides, the pattern can be used twice. An example of this is the pattern of a cabriole leg as shown in Illus. 6-2. A clear $^1/_8$" Plexiglas template is used to lay out the pattern.

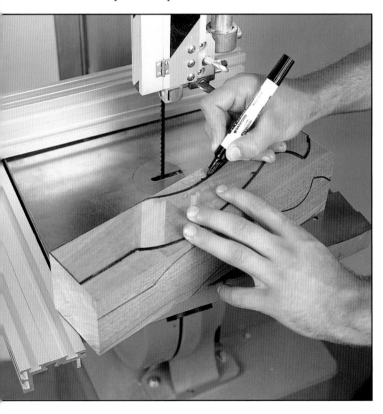

Illus. 6-2. A Plexiglas® template is used to mark the adjacent sides on a cabriole leg.

• Compound Sawing

When there is a pattern on adjacent sides, two series or cuts are needed to release the workpiece. The cabriole leg shown in Chapter 4 is an example.

Templates

Paper patterns are not very durable. If you are going to use a pattern often, it is worthwhile to make a template from a durable material such as fiberboard, plywood, or Plexiglas. Then use the template to trace the pattern directly onto the workpiece. A clear Plexiglas template works well because you can see the grain of the wood through it. Templates are useful on some large workpieces where part of the pattern can be drawn on opposite sides of the workpiece.

Pattern Sawing

Pattern sawing is a technique used to make multiple pieces that are identical. A solid template is attached to the workpiece. It works best if the template is made of plywood, because plywood, unlike solid wood, is stable—it does not shrink or expand. The waste material is removed with the band saw cut near to, but not touching, the template. The rest of the waste is removed with a router bit.

Pattern sawing and routing are efficient techniques for making multiple identical pieces such as table or chair parts. Pattern sawing is easy. Take your time and make a good template. A good example of pattern sawing and routing is the chair back as shown in Illus. 6-3 on opposite page. The rail has a curve on the top; the front and the back of it are curved. If possible, always do the joinery when the stock is in the square form. The tenon is formed on the end of the workpiece as shown in Illus. 6-4 and Illus. 6-5 on opposite page.

Illus. 6-3. This chair back has a curved top and has a parallel curve on the front and the back.

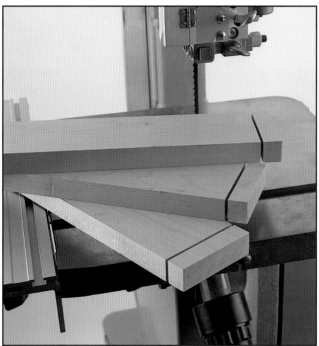

Illus. 6-4. Do the joinery before the curves are cut on the band saw. The tenon shoulders for the chair backs are crosscut on the table saw before being completed on the band saw.

Illus. 6-5. The tenons are cut on the band saw. This technique is discussed in detail in Chapter 8.

Clamp a rub block to the band saw table or rip fence as shown in Illus. 6-6. The rub block should have a curved end with a notch in it. The notch fits over the blade, extending past it about $^1/_{16}$".

Tape the plywood template to the workpiece with double-sided tape. The template will contact the rub block during the cut as shown in Illus. 6-7 and Illus. 6-8.

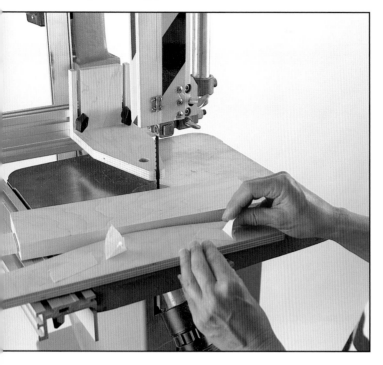

Illus. 6-6. Clamp a rub block to the band saw table or rip fence.

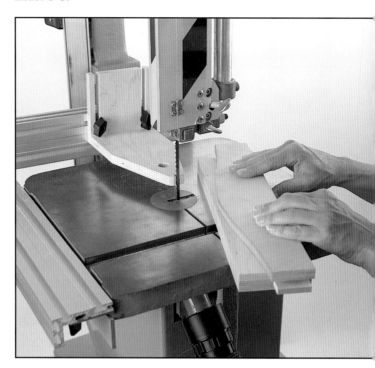

Illus. 6-7. Attach the template with double-sided tape. Avoid using too much tape or it will be difficult to get the template off.

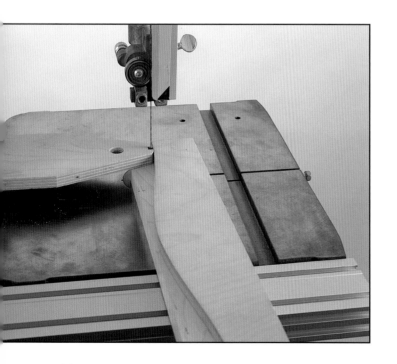

Illus. 6-8. Clamp the rub block to the table or the rip fence. The notch in the rub block fits over the blade and protrudes past it by about $^1/_{16}$".

Because the blade is about $^1/_{16}$" short of the template, the workpiece extends past the template about $^1/_{16}$" as shown in Illus. 6-9 and Illus. 6-10 on opposite page. An alternative to the use of the rip fence is a rub block clamped to the table as shown in Illus. 6-11 on opposite page.

Illus. 6-9. Begin the cut with the template touching the rub block. As you continue cutting, use slight pressure to keep the template against the rub block.

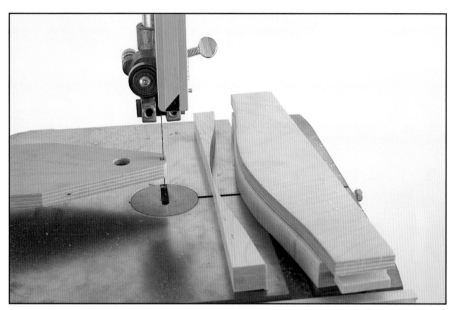

Illus. 6-10. The complete cut. The workpiece should extend about $1/16$" past the template.

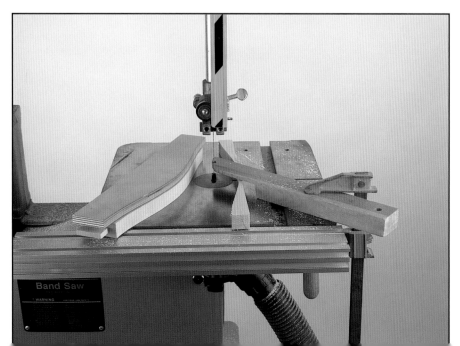

Illus. 6-11. This rub block is clamped to the table. A cutout allows the waste to pass under the rub block.

Trim away the $1/16$" waste with a router table and a flush-trimming router bit. A flush-trimming router bit is a bit with a bearing on top of it. The bearing rubs against the template as the router trims the waste. The finish is smooth and requires little sanding as shown in Illus. 6-12 and Illus. 6-13. The jig that is used to hold the chair back is a half pattern. It is held in place with two fast-action clamps. Half of the pattern is routed and then the piece is unclamped and the other half is routed. The advantage with this design is that the router bit is always trimming with the grain, avoiding any tear-out or chipping.

To make the parallel curves, another template is used. This is a rectangular board with a $3/16$" curve cut in it as shown in Illus. 6-14.

Illus. 6-13. A close-up of the flush-trimming router bit. This jig should be used with a starting pin shown to the left of the router bit. The bearing on the bottom of the bit contacts the jig.

Illus. 6-12. The flush-trimming router bit trims off the waste. The workpiece is clamped in a half-pattern jig. The router table is used for this operation. The bearing on the bottom of the bit rides against the curved template on the jig. A half-pattern jig holds the workpiece while you rout half of the shape. Release the clamps, turn the workpiece over end for end, and cut the second part of the curve.

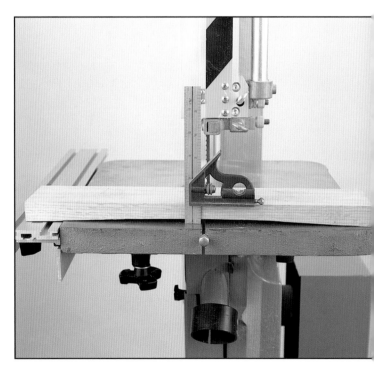

Illus. 6-14. A curved template is used to make the initial curve on the back of the chair slat. The center of the curve measures in $3/16$".

48

The workpiece is attached to the template with double-sided tape, similar to the way that the pattern was attached, as shown in Illus. 6-15.

The template rests against a curved rip fence or a rectangular spacer block attached as shown in Illus. 6-16.

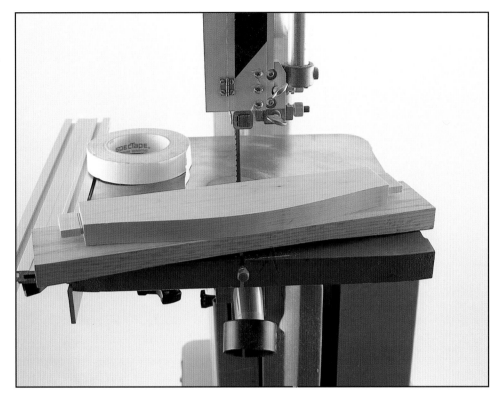

Illus. 6-15. The chair slat is attached to the straight side of the template with double-sided tape.

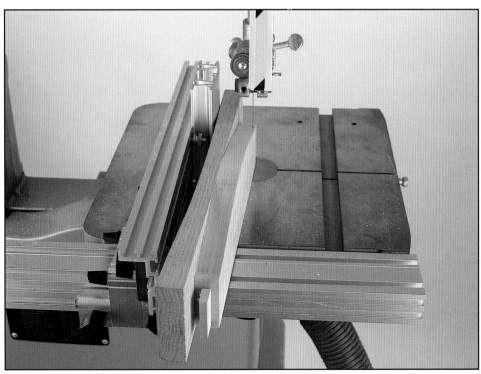

Illus. 6-16. A 2" spacer block is attached to the rip fence with double-sided tape. The center of the spacer block should be aligned with the saw blade. If available, a curved aluminum rip fence can be used.

The cut is made and then the workpiece is rotated and flipped for the second cut as shown in Illus. 6-17 and Illus. 6-18. Both the curved template and the workpiece are clamped in a vise and the band saw surface is planed smooth as shown in Illus. 6-19 and Illus. 6-20.

Illus. 6-17. The workpiece is fed into the blade and a tapered waste piece is removed.

Illus. 6-19. The workpiece is cleaned up with a plane.

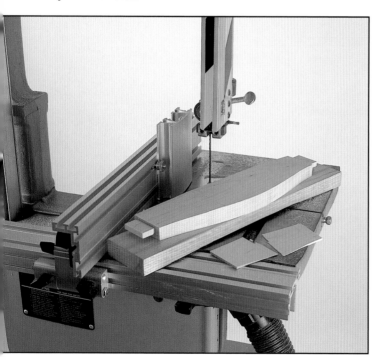

Illus. 6-18. The workpiece is rotated and then fed into the blade. The opposite tapered waste piece is removed.

Illus. 6-20. The completed back side.

50

For the inside curve of the chair back, the workpiece is cut freehand against the rip fence using the planed curve on the chair back as a guide. The workpiece contacts the rip fence about $^1/4$" in front of

the blade as it is cut as shown in Illus. 6-21 and Illus. 6-22.

The inside curve is finished with a compass plane as shown in Illus. 6-23.

Illus. 6-21. The planed curve on the chair back is used as a guide to cut the inside curve of the chair back by contacting the rip fence about $^1/4$" in front of the blade.

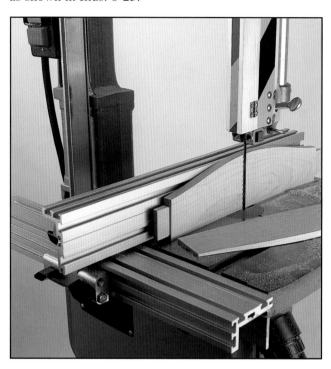

Illus. 6-22. The waste is thicker in the center and thinner on the outside.

Illus. 6-23. Finish the concave side with a technique that matches your skill level. A compass plane is the ideal tool for this situation.

CHAPTER 7

jigs and fixtures

The terms jigs and fixtures are often used interchangeably or together to define a store bought accessory or something that you can make yourself for your shop. A jig is defined as a fixture that also serves as a tool guide. A fixture is defined as a device that positions or holds the work. The idea behind jigs and fixtures is that one of these devices will help you work more efficiently and more accurately.

Designing and building jigs and fixtures is an acquired skill—the more you do it, the more you will learn how to do it. The trick is to see the big picture—if you can find and define the problem, it is easier to design a good solution.

The purpose of this chapter is to give you some ideas for jigs and fixtures that can speed up your work and make it more accurate. The best jig is the one that you do not need, meaning that you can often do things with what you already have, such as a miter slot or a rip fence.

Jigs for the band saw are fairly simple. A good example is the taper jig as shown in Illus. 7-1.

It is an angled board with a dowel in it. The dowel acts as a stop, positioning the workpiece as the entire unit is moved past the blade.

Jigs for Pattern Sawing and Routing

Pattern sawing and routing is covered in Chapter 6. The template is attached to the top of the workpiece with double-sided tape. With the help of a template and a rub block, the shape is rough-cut with the band saw. The final, smooth shape is created by the ball-bearing flush-trimming router bit removing the excess waste.

For making multiple pieces such as chair backs, it is easier to make a template and clamp the workpiece to it. In this situation, a flush-trimming router bit with the bearing on the bottom of the bit works best.

With curved work, the grain of the wood introduces a problem you do not have when sawing straight boards. Routing against the grain almost always guarantees tear-out. To avoid tear-out, try to rout with the grain. Usually half of the shape will be cut with the grain and the other half will be cut against the grain.

When you want to rout a symmetrical part, use a half-pattern jig, as shown in Illus. 6-12 on page 48. Because you do not want to rout the entire profile at once, you do not need to make a template for the entire shape.

Illus. 7-1. This simple taper jig is made from a tapered board and dowel.

Remember to cut the tenons first. Cut out the curve of the template, then sand or plane it to shape. Ideally the template should extend quite a ways on each side of the workpiece. Rough-cut the shape on the band saw and clamp the workpiece into the jig. Using a starting pin, begin the cut on the flat part of the jig with the grain. When half of the shape is done, flip the workpiece over and trim the waste off the other half.

Circular Work

Many projects require either complete circles or a portion of a circle. Although it is possible to cut a circle freehand, it is not the most accurate way. The most accurate way would be to use a circle-cutting jig. The basic idea is to position a rotation point at a given distance from the blade. As the workpiece rotates on the point, the circle is cut. The work is rotated around a point similar to the way a compass rotates around a central point. The distance between the point and the blade determines the radius of the circle. The rotation point is held in place by the jig.

Circle-cutting jigs are commercially available or can be shop-made—both work the same way. Commercial jigs are usually adjustable so that you can easily change the radius of the circle. The rotation point can be either above or below the workpiece. Having the rotation point on the bottom has some advantages, especially if you use the jig for cutting half and quarter circles.

The jig slides in the miter slot until its forward motion is limited by a stop nut.

To use the jig, do the following:

1. Locate the center of the workpiece; then make a hole for the rotation point and mount the workpiece onto the point as shown in Illus. 7-2.

2. Position the stop nut on the jig at the appropriate radius as shown in Illus. 7-3.

3. Position the point in the center of the board as shown in Illus.7-4.

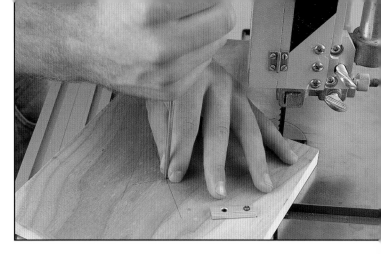

Illus. 7-2. Puncture a small hole into the center of the workpiece.

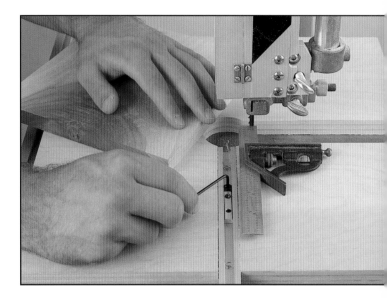

Illus. 7-3. Position the nut which stops the forward movement of the pin toward the blade.

Illus. 7-4. Hammer the pin into the center hole, then position the pin on the extrusion of the circle jig.

53

4. Set the jig stop so the forward movement of the jig stops with the pin lined up exactly with the front of the blade. Move the jig and the workpiece into the blade until the jig stop touches the table. The adjustable stop block must stay in contact with the table or the cut will not be round. Slowly rotate the workpiece on the point until the circle is completed as shown in Illus. 7-5 and Illus. 7-6.

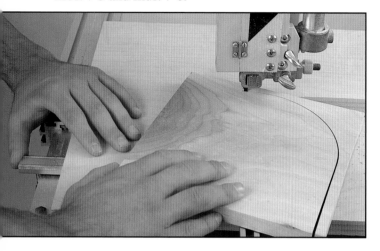

Illus. 7-5. The jig slides in the miter slot. Keep forward pressure on the jig and pressure on the workpiece toward the blade as the piece is rotated. When using the bottom pivot point, move the jig and workpiece forward to create a straight line. When the rotation point is even with the front of the saw blade, rotate the work to create the circle. The adjustable stop block clamped to the miter slot runner should contact the table as the front of the blade touches the radius line.

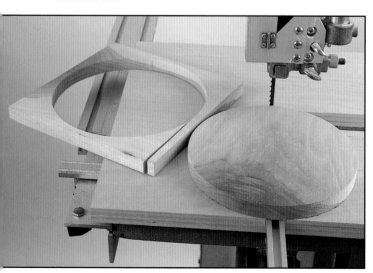

Illus. 7-6. The completed circle.

54

A circle-cutting jig is particularly useful for wood turners. The closer a workpiece is to a circle, the less material must be removed with a turning tool on the lathe. It also decreases the amount of vibration. To flatten the bottom of a rough board, use a power plane as shown in Illus. 7-7. A hand plane can also be used.

Position the workpiece on the circle-cutting jig with the table tilted at the desired angle as shown in Illus. 7-8.

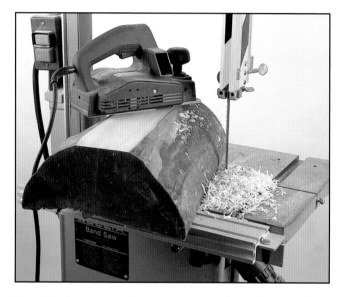

Illus. 7-7. Large rough pieces can be cut on the circle-cutting jig if the bottom is flattened with a plane.

Illus. 7-8. Position the piece on the pin and advance it into the blade until the forward motion of the jig is stopped.

Try to position the workpiece on the jig so that it is properly centered. Ideally, the saw blade should trim off the edge as shown in Illus. 7-9.

The completed circle will have a smooth side wall and be well-balanced with only the top retaining its rough characteristics as shown in Illus. 7-10. Trimming the waste on a band saw saves time and energy. It is also safer than turning an unbalanced piece on the lathe.

Illus. 7-9. Rotate the wood to create the circle.

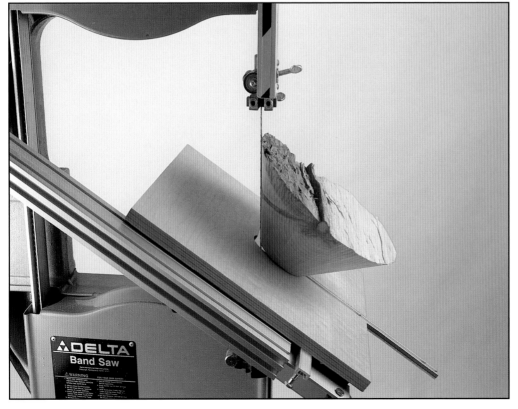

Illus. 7-10. The completed circle.

Radius Jigs

Radius jigs are useful for making partial circles. The radius jig rests on top of the circle jig. You can easily make a radius jig by attaching two strips of wood to each side of a completed piece. The radius jig sits on top of the rotation point. A half-circle jig is very useful for production items as shown in Illus. 7-11 and Illus. 7-12. A radius jig is also useful for quarter circles.

This will save the effort of having to mark, punch, and position each corner. Simply hold the workpiece against the radius jig sides and rotate the jig. It is important that the circle-cutting jig does not move during this operation, and for this reason, you may want to clamp it to the table. You can also use the radius jig in conjunction with a sanding belt to sand the corners.

A radius jig is easy to use because the workpiece can be held in the corner without the need for a clamp as shown in Illus. 7-13.

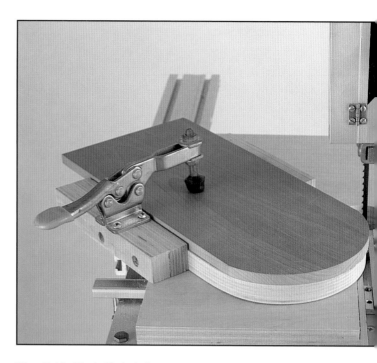

Illus. 7-12. The half-circle jig rests on top of the circle-cutting jig.

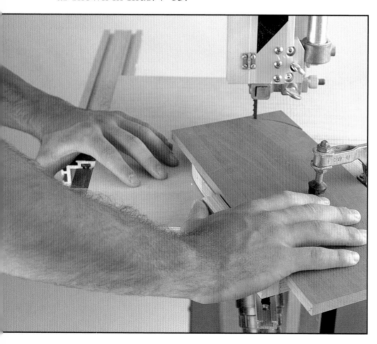

Illus. 7-11. The half-circle jig consists of a piece of plywood with strips of plywood nailed to its sides. An adjustable clamp is used to hold the workpiece during the saw cut.

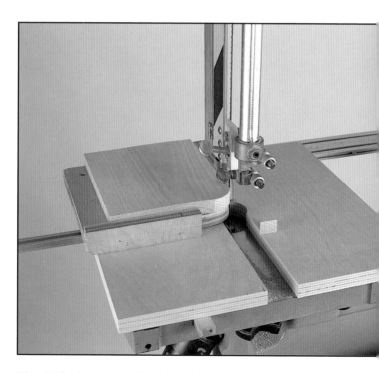

Illus. 7-13. A quarter-circle cut is usually referred to as a radius cut. Place the work on the circle-cutting jig point and rotate the piece into the saw blade, thus making a quarter circle. Make a radius jig by adding a wood strip to each side. Hold the workpiece in the corner of the jig and make the cut. You can make the cut without having to measure, mark, or punch a hole.

joinery

Cutting Tenons

The mortise and tenon joint and the dovetail joint are the two strongest joints. The mortise and tenon joint is used for framework such as chairs and tables. The dovetail joint is usually used for carcass work such as drawers and cabinets.

With the advent of powerful plunger routers, it is now easier to make the mortise. The mortise made with a router requires a tenon that will fit the rounded corner left by the router bit. The solution is to design a tenon that will fit the round mortise. One solution is to make the tenon corners angled. This solves the problem of fitting a square tenon to a round corner. It also solves the problem of releasing glue pressure. The 45° corner will snugly fit the rounded corner, but it will also allow for the escape of captured glue. This is the idea behind the fluted dowel.

The tenon requires two types of cuts. A crosscut is used to define the shoulder of the tenon. This can be done on the band saw, but it is often done on the table saw. After the crosscut is made, a rip cut is used to define the tenon. The band saw excels at this type of cutting because of its ability to cut into a corner.

Another advantage is that the workpiece lays flat on the table for this process rather than having an end straight up in the air, as is the case when the table saw is used. It is often better to crosscut with the table saw so that the crosscut is slightly ($1/32$") deeper than the rip cut. This ensures that the corner cut will be complete and provides a place for the excess glue.

The setup for doing the rip cut is the usual setup for ripping. Using a microadjusting jig facilitates the final fitting of the joint. Cut the mortise first, then fit the tenon to it as shown in Illus. 8-1 and Illus. 8-2.

Illus. 8-1. The tenon requires two series of cuts. Crosscut the shoulder first with a table saw. Here the progression of these cuts is shown. The setup for cutting the tenons is like that for making a rip cut. Make the first series of cuts.

Illus. 8-2. Fit the tenon to the mortise.

Next, make the other shoulder cut as shown in Illus. 8-3. This is the less critical of the cuts, especially if the mortise is round. A stop on the track prevents you from accidentally cutting into the stock. Then fit the tenon to the mortise as shown in Illus. 8-4. Remember to leave some room for the glue.

If you have a rounded mortise, you will want to bevel the corners. Tilt the table to 45° or make a fixture to hold the tenon on a 45° angle as shown in Illus. 8-5 and Illus. 8-6. Make the bevel cuts by cutting the opposite corners with the same rip fence setting.

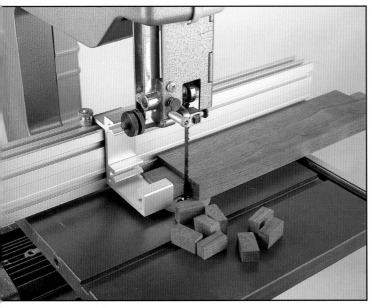

Illus. 8-3. Lay the piece flat on the table and make the other shoulder cut. Use a stop block to stop the cut. If you use a rip fence with a microadjuster, you will be able to easily make a tight fit.

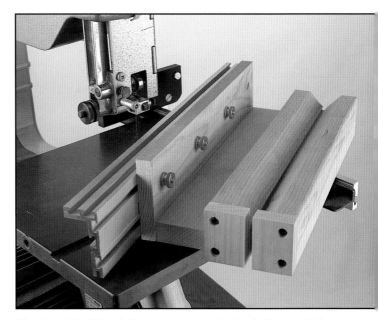

Illus. 8-5. The V-block jig is an example of a simple fixture which can be used for a variety of purposes.

Illus. 8-4. Fit the tenon to the mortise.

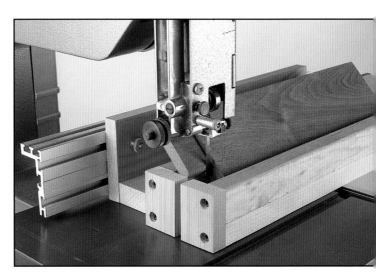

Illus. 8-6. If the mortise was done with a router the corners will be round. The V-block jig will help you to accurately cut off the tenon corner so that the tenon will fit into a rounded mortise. The flat surfaces allow for a glue release that is similar to the flutes on a dowel.

Cutting Dovetails

Dovetails are created with a series of straight-angled cuts with a dovetail taper jig and a series of spacer blocks. A ⅛" blade is used to cut and remove the waste. For maximum accuracy, nonmetal blocks should be adjusted next to the blade. The taper jig determines the 10° angle of the dovetail and the spacer blocks very accurately space the cuts as shown in Illus. 8-7.

Prepare the dovetail stock by putting a sharp gauge line on the wood with a marking gauge to create a sharp knife line. The sharp knife line should be the same distance from the edge of the board as the thickness of the stock as shown in Illus. 8-8.

The pin and half-pin sizes are determined by the difference between the workpiece and the measuring blocks. Put the blocks next to the workpiece and mark the starting line with a pencil as shown in Illus. 8-9.

Illus. 8-8. Prepare the dovetail stock by putting a sharp gauge line on the wood with a marking gauge to create a sharp knife line. The sharp knife line should be the same distance from the edge of the board as the thickness of the stock.

Illus. 8-7. Dovetails are created with a series of angle cuts using spacing blocks and a jig. The jig determines the 10° angle and the spacing blocks accurately space the cuts. A ⅛" blade is used to cut and remove the waste. For maximum accuracy, Cool Blocks should be adjusted next to the blade.

Illus. 8-9. The pin and half-pin sizes are determined by the difference between the workpiece and the measuring blocks. Put the blocks next the workpiece and mark the starting line with a pencil.

Place the blocks on the taper jig and move the fence to align the saw blade with the pencil mark. Make a cut down to the knife line, then set a stop block to stop the forward movement of the jig as shown in Illus. 8-10. Cut all four corners, then remove one spacer block and repeat the series of four cuts, rotating and turning the board end for end as shown in Illus. 8-11.

An $^1/_8"$ of material is wasted to make space for the blade. The material in the pin area will be wasted with with the $^1/_8"$. Slide the board laterally and make a series of cuts to remove the material as shown in Illus. 8-12.

Because you want to cut the gauge line in half, you have to accurately adjust the rip fence as shown in Illus. 8-13. Some saw rip fences are fitted with an optional microadjuster which is ideal for making dovetails. Test the rip fence position on scrap.

Illus. 8-10. Place the blocks on the taper jig and move the fence to align the saw blade with the pencil mark. Make a cut down to the knife line, then set a stop block to stop the forward movement of the jig.

Illus. 8-12. An $^1/_8"$ of material is wasted to make space for the blade. The material in the pin area will be wasted with the $^1/_8"$. Slide the board laterally and make a series of cuts to remove the material.

Illus. 8-11. Cut all four corners, then remove one spacer block and repeat the series of four cuts, rotating and turning the board end for end.

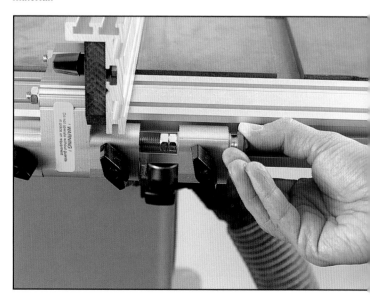

Illus. 8-13. Some saw rip fences are fitted with an optional microadjuster which is ideal for accurate work such as making dovetails.

Slide the tail board into the blade to remove the half-pin waste as shown in Illus. 8-14.

To remove the pin waste, slide the blade into the wide kerf and remove the waste as shown in Illus. 8-15. Rotate the board and cut into the opposite corner to clean out the space between the tails.

After the tails are completed, the pins are made with two series of cuts with the table tilted at 10°. The first series is made with the table tilted in one direction and then the second series is made with the table tilted in the opposite direction. To make the first cut, line up the rip fence so the tail piece is lined up with the blade as shown in Illus. 8-16. Line up the tail so the blade will cut into the corner of the tail. Make the cut on the pin board.

Illus. 8-15. To remove the pin waste, slide the blade into the wide kerf and remove the waste. Rotate the board and cut into the opposite corner to clean out the space between the tails.

Illus. 8-14. Slide the tail board into the blade to remove the half pin-waste.

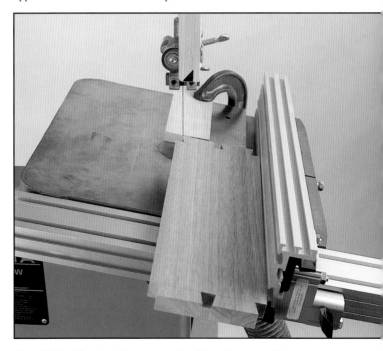

Illus. 8-16. After the tails are completed the pins are made by two series of cuts with the table tilted at 10° degrees. The first series is made with the table tilted to the right. Line up the rip fence so the tail piece is lined up with the blade. Line up the tail so the blade will cut into the corner of the tail. Make the cut on the pin board.

61

Make the first cut in opposite corners of the workpiece. For the second series, add a spacing block and then make another series of cuts as shown in Illus. 8-17. Tilt the table 10° in the opposite direction and repeat the process as shown in Illus. 8-18.

Illus. 8-19 shows the sequencial steps in making the pins.

Illus. 8-20 shows the completed dovetail.

Illus. 8-17. Make the first cut in opposite corners of the workpiece. For the second series add a spacing block, then make another series of cuts.

Illus. 8-19. This shows the sequential steps in making the pins.

Illus. 8-18. Tilt the table 10° in the opposite direction and repeat the process.

Illus. 8-20. The completed dovetail.

artists' projects

Oak Candlesticks, oak, 12" high x 3³/₄" wide

Oak Candlesticks
Designed by Seth Anderson

These candlesticks are made from a single weathered oak 4 x 4. They can be made on the band saw in a variety of shapes and sizes. You can easily change the size and the design to fit the size of blank you have. You can also enhance the design with cuts made by the table saw or router table.

The candlestick shown on the right was made from a squared piece. The stock was jointed and then planed so it was square. The candlestick shown on the left was made from the same 4 x 4, but the weathered outside was left intact.

Construction:

1.   Lay the pattern out on all four sides of the wood, using the Oak Candlestick Pattern below.

2.   Make all the crosscuts with a rip fence.

Note: You can clamp a stop to the table so all crosscuts will be the same depth.

3.   After all crosscuts are completed, start making the angled cuts on each end.

Note: The square corners on each end add character, but also keep a square surface on the band saw table.

*Oak Candlestick Pattern
(side view)*

12"

Oak Arts & Crafts Lamp

Designed by Mark Duginske

This table lamp was designed to fit into a room with Arts & Crafts furniture. The traditional wood for Arts & Crafts furniture is oak. This lamp is made from red oak that was selectively harvested from my land and air-dried in a barn for eight years.

The lamp shade was purchased at a lighting store; the lamp parts were purchased at a hardware store. It may be a good idea to purchase the lamp shade first, then adjust the size of the lamp base accordingly.

The grain of the wood is accentuated with medium-colored wood filler and stained with honey maple gel stain. It was then finished with poly gel.

Although this lamp was designed as a table lamp, it could be elongated and enlarged to be a floor lamp.

Construction:

1. Make the lamp base from two pieces of wood $11^{1}/_{2}$" long, $1^{5}/_{8}$" thick, and $1^{7}/_{8}$" wide.

2. Cut the $^{5}/_{8}$" open area with the band saw.

3. Cut a lap joint on the table saw and fit the pieces together.

4. Drill a hole in the center of the lap joint to accommodate the electrical cord.

5. Make the column from two pieces of $^{3}/_{4}$"-square oak that are dadoed to accommodate the electrical cord before gluing.

6. Secure the column to the lamp base with two wood screws.

7. You will need to make four curved supports. To do this efficiently and to guarantee the size, make a jig to do the final shaping on the router table. This technique is shown in detail in Chapter 7.

Note: Ideally the four supports should be exactly the same size or the piece will look out of balance.

Oak Arts & Crafts Lamp, red oak, 14" high x 11$^{1}/_{2}$" wide

8. Make a pine template, using the Oak Arts & Crafts Lamp Support Pattern at right.

9. Temporarily screw the template to the jig base.

10. Screw the location stops to the jig base and add a mechanism. In this case, a piece of standard track was secured to the jig base and a piece of plywood was added as a clamp board to secure the small oak pieces as shown in Illus. 9-1.

11. Cut the jig base and the clamp board along the contour of the template with the band saw, leaving about $^1/_{16}$" to $^1/_8$" of plywood proud of the template.

12. Trim the jig base and the clamp board to the exact shape of the template with a flush-trimming router bit.

13. Remove the template from the jig base. Trace the design on each oak piece, using the template as a pattern.

14. Insert each oak piece into the jig and cut out each support with the band saw, leaving about $^1/_{16}$" to be trimmed off.

15. Trim each support with a flush-trimming router bit.

16. Glue the supports to the corners between the lamp base and the column.

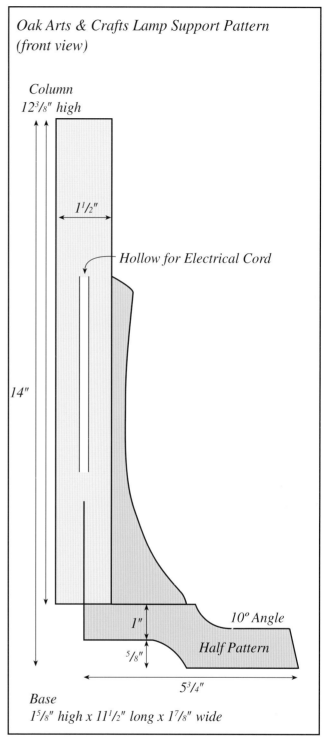

Oak Arts & Crafts Lamp Support Pattern (front view)

Column 12$^3/_8$" high

1$^1/_2$"

Hollow for Electrical Cord

14"

1"

$^5/_8$"

10° Angle

Half Pattern

5$^3/_4$"

Base 1$^5/_8$" high x 11$^1/_2$" long x 1$^7/_8$" wide

Illus. 9-1. There are four curved supports glued to the corner between the base and the column. To make the supports efficiently and to guarantee the size, a jig was made to do the final shaping on the router table. The supports are trimmed with a flush-trimming router bit after they are sized with the band saw.

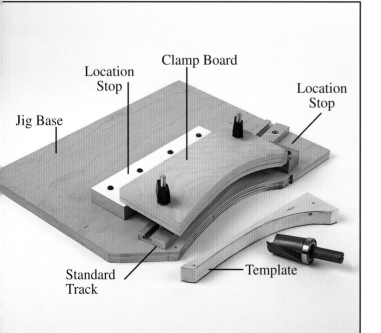

Location Stop

Clamp Board

Location Stop

Jig Base

Standard Track

Template

Three Leg Lamp, red oak, 13¹/₄" high x 9¹/₂" wide

Three Leg Lamp

Designed by Mark Duginske

This lamp is made from red oak that was selectively harvested from my land and air dried in a barn for eight years.

The lamp shade was purchased at a lighting store; the lamp parts were purchased at a hardware store. It may be a good idea to purchase the lamp shade first, then adjust the size of the lamp base accordingly.

The grain of the wood is accentuated with medium-colored wood filler and stained with honey maple gel stain. It was then finished with poly gel.

Although this lamp was designed as a table lamp, it could be elongated and enlarged to be a floor lamp.

Construction:

1. Make the lamp base from three identical pieces of wood 13¹/₄" long, ³/₄" thick, and 5¹/₂" wide.

2. Lay the mating side flat on the table saw and cut with the blade tilted to a 30° angle.

3. Drill a hole in the middle of the three pieces of wood with a ³/₈" round core box bit on the router table to accommodate the lamp hardware and electrical cord.

4. You will need to make three curved legs. To do this efficiently and to guarantee the size, make a jig to do the final shaping on the router table. This technique is shown in detail in Chapter 7.

Note: Ideally the three legs should be exactly the same size or the piece will look out of balance.

5. Make a pine template, using the Three Leg Lamp Pattern on page 67.

6. Temporarily screw the template to the jig base.

7. Screw the location stops to the jig base and add a mechanism. In this case, clamps were used to secure the small oak pieces as shown in Illus. 9-2.

8. Cut the jig base along the contour of the template with the band saw, leaving about $^1/_{16}$" to $^1/_8$" of plywood proud of the template.

9. Trim the jig base to the exact shape of the template with a flush-trimming router bit.

10. Remove the template from the jig base. Draw a design on each oak piece, using the template as a pattern.

11. Place each oak piece onto the jig and clamp down to secure. Cut out each leg with the band saw, leaving about $^1/_{16}$" to be trimmed off. This jig has two curved surfaces so it can be used to cut the outside and the bottom of the leg.

12. Trim each leg with a flush-trimming router bit.

13. Glue the three legs together and hold in place with large rubber bands until the glue has dried.

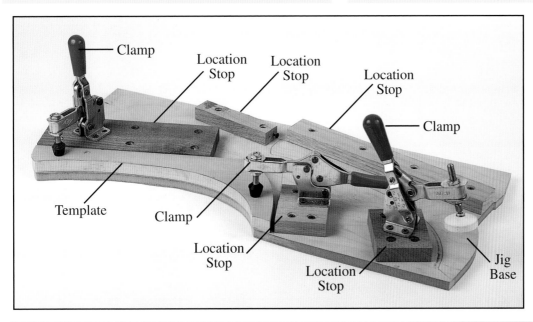

Illus. 9-2. To make the legs efficiently and to guarantee the size, a jig was made to do the final shaping on the router table. This jig has two curved surfaces so it can be used to cut the outside and the bottom of the leg. A flush-trimming router bit trims the small oak pieces after they are sized on the band saw.

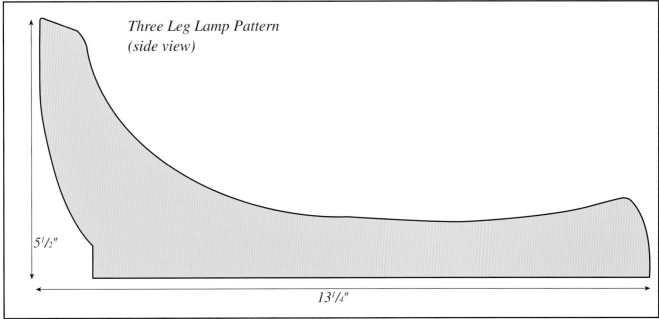

Three Leg Lamp Pattern (side view)

$5^1/_2$"

$13^1/_4$"

Walnut Shelf

Designed by Mary Kleinschmidt

This shelf is made from walnut. It features three full-sized shelves and a top shelf that is slightly narrower. The thin shelves give this design a light feeling.

The decorative sides are typical of work done by Scandinavian immigrants.

A simple geometric design is carved into the sides of the shelf to add interest.

The shelf was then finished with a clear oil finish.

The shelf is quite small and can easily be scaled up.

Construction:

1.   Make the shelves from wood 26" long, $^1/_4$" thick, and $12^1/_2$" wide.

2.   Make the sides from wood 26" long, $^1/_2$" thick, and $5^1/_8$" wide.

Note: Do not cut the pattern in the sides until the shelves have been dadoed into the sides.

3.   Tape or screw the two sides together and cut out the decorative edges, using the Walnut Shelf Pattern on page 69. Make certain that the dadoes are in alignment.

Note: Cutting both sides at the same time guarantees that the sides will be symmetrical.

4.   If desired, carve the geometric design into the sides.

5.   Assemble the shelf.

Walnut Shelf, walnut, $25^1/_2$" high x $12^1/_2$" wide x $^1/_2$" thick

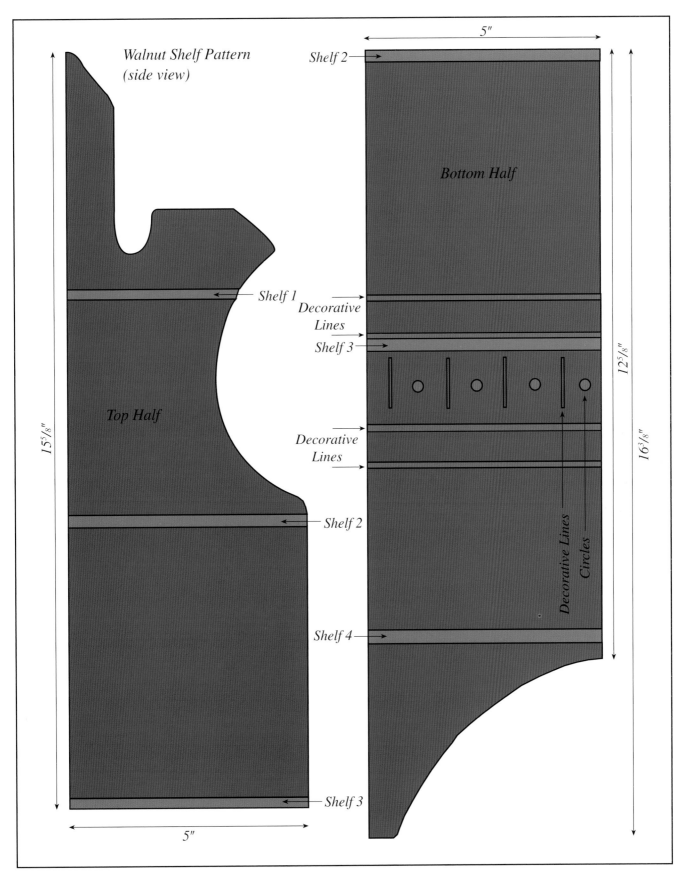

Walnut Shelf Pattern (side view)

Corner Shelf, stained white pine, 29" high x 6¹/₄" wide x ⁵/₈" thick

Corner Shelf

Designed by Mary Kleinschmidt

This shelf is made from white pine and then stained with walnut gel stain. It features three circular shelves.

The decorative sides are typical of work done by Scandinavian immigrants.

The shelf is 29" high so it will accommodate small- to medium-sized objects nicely. The pattern can easily be scaled up or down.

Construction:

1. Make the shelves from wood 9" long, ¹/₂" thick, and 6¹/₄" wide. Because the shelves have a circular shape, they are easily cut with a circle-cutting jig. This technique is shown in detail in Chapter 7.

2. Make the sides from wood 29" long, ¹/₂" thick, and 7¹/₄" wide.

Note: Do not cut the pattern in the sides until the shelves have been dadoed into the sides.

3. Tape or screw the two sides together and cut out the decorative edges, using the Corner Shelf Pattern on page 71. Make certain that the dadoes are in alignment.

Note: Cutting both sides at the same time guarantees that the sides will be symmetrical.

4. Assemble the shelf.

Note: The shelves can be screwed in place from the back of the shelf.

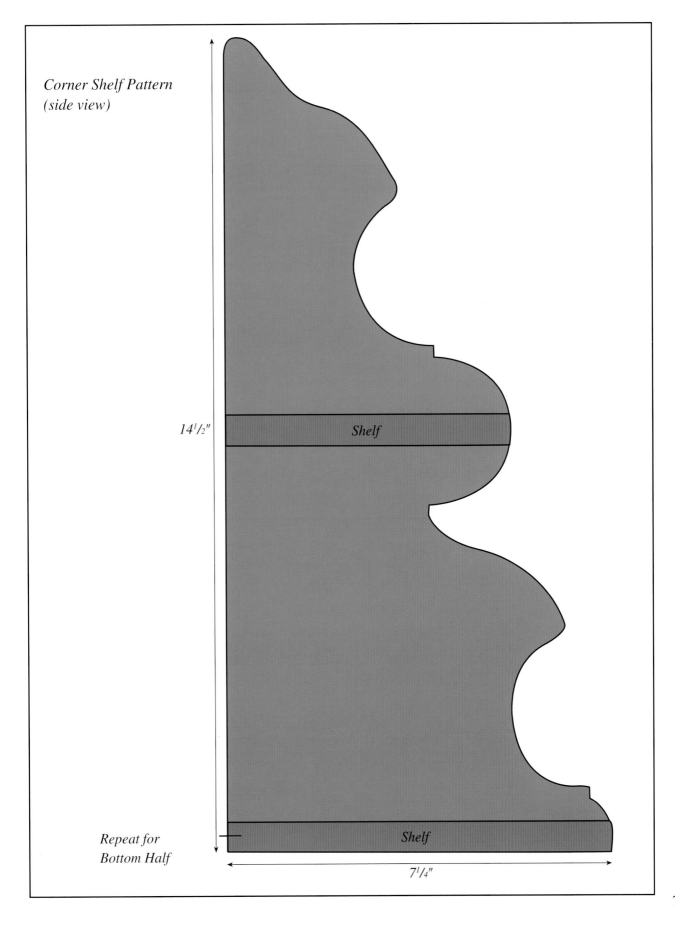

Corner Shelf Pattern
(side view)

$14^1/_2''$

Shelf

Shelf

Repeat for
Bottom Half

$7^1/_4''$

*Mantel Clock,
walnut,
14¹/₂" long x
6³/₄" wide x
2¹/₂" thick*

Mantel Clock

Designed by Jeff Harris

This clock is made from a single piece of walnut and finished with varnish.

The clock mechanism was purchased through a mail-order catalog. It may be a good idea to purchase the clock mechanism first, then adjust the size of the clock accordingly. Most clock mechanisms are battery operated and are usually compact in size.

Although this clock was designed as for the mantel, it could be made smaller for a desk clock.

Construction:

1. Make the clock from wood 14$\frac{1}{2}$" long, 2$\frac{1}{2}$" thick, and 6$\frac{3}{4}$" wide, using a band saw with a circle-cutting jig and using the Mantel Clock Pattern on page 73.

2. To install the clock mechanism, drill a hole in the front center of the clock to accommodate the mechanism. If you are using an adjustable drill bit, make a test hole on a piece of scrap wood.

Note: As with all hardware, it is a good idea not to start a project until you have received and studied it.

3. Pressure-fit the clock mechanism into the drilled opening so it can be easily removed to change the battery.

4. To do the finish work with a flush-trimming router bit, review Chapters 6 and 7.

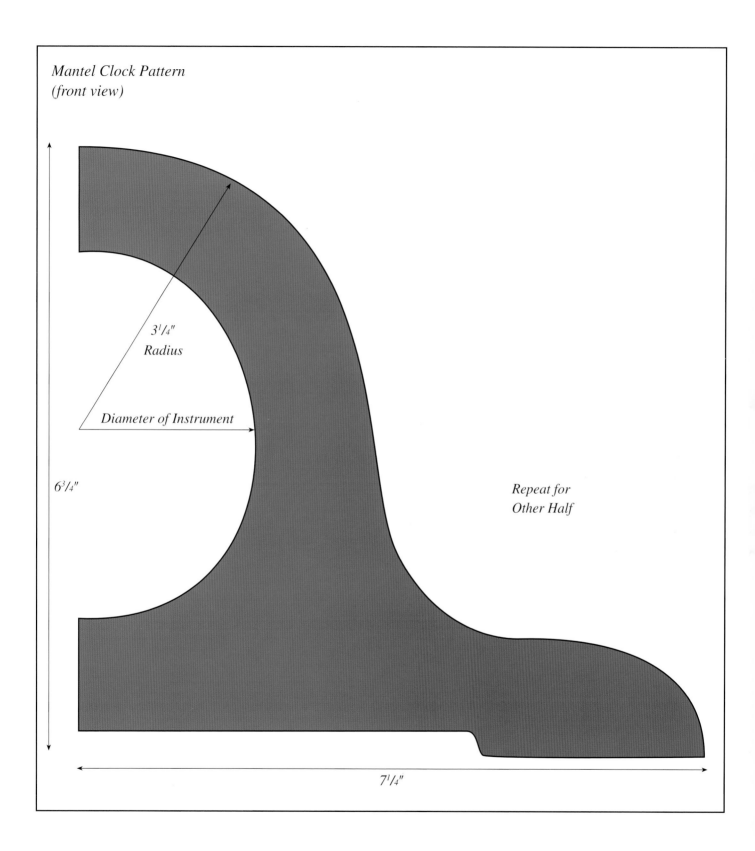

Mantel Clock Pattern
(front view)

$3^1/_4"$
Radius

Diameter of Instrument

$6^3/_4"$

Repeat for
Other Half

$7^1/_4"$

Tree, walnut, 6¹/₂" high x 5¹/₂" wide x ³/₄" thick

Tree
Designed by Liz Edwards

This tree is made from a single piece of walnut then finished with a clear oil. It is a simple design that uses a simple technique.

This technique provides dramatic results for a minimum cost in time and materials and can be used with a variety of shapes. It is particularly useful when making holiday decorations.

Construction:

1. Make the tree from wood 6¹/₂" long, ³/₄" thick, and 5¹/₂" wide, using the Tree Pattern on page 75.

2. To make the cuts, tilt the table and use a ¹/₁₆" blade.

Note: Replace the metal guides with Cool Blocks to use the ¹/₆" band saw blade. This technique could also be used on a scroll saw.

3. If necessary, refer to the Intarsia Chart on page 28 to determine how much to tilt the table in relationship to the width of the blade.

Note: Experiment with scrap wood to see exactly how much to tilt the table for the particular blade you have in your saw.

4. As the elements are moved, the pieces of the tree lock in place. For easy storage, the pieces are shoved back together to a flat position.

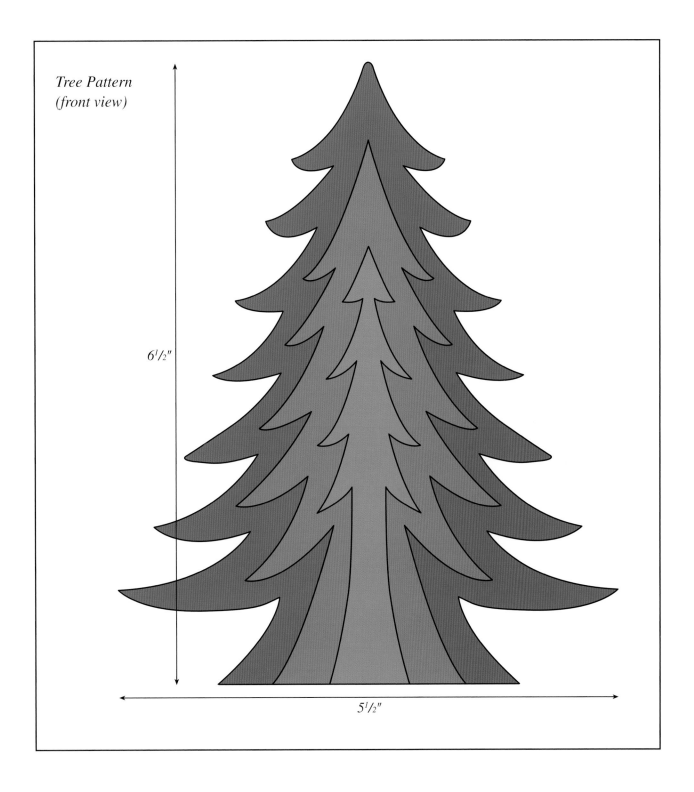

*Tree Pattern
(front view)*

6¹/₂"

5¹/₂"

Adjustable Book Ends

Designed by Gene Duginske

These adjustable book ends are made from oak and will support a number of books on a table or other flat surface.

Because these book ends are adjustable, dowels are used to secure the decorative ends to the base, allowing them to be easily moved.

Construction:

1. Make the book end base from wood 9" long, ³/₄" thick, and 5¹/₂" wide, using the Book End Base Pattern on page 77.

2. Make the decorative ends from two pieces of wood 7" long, ³/₄" thick, and 5¹/₂" wide, using the Book End Decorative End Pattern on page 77.

3. To make each decorative end, glue two pieces of wood together. Then cut the "half pattern" out of the piece of wood.

Note: This technique offers the advantage of insuring that both sides are symmetrical.

4. Glue the two halves together to create the decorative pattern of the book ends.

5. Drill holes in the book end base and in the decorative ends as shown on the patterns to accommodate the dowels.

6. Secure the decorative ends to the book end base with dowels.

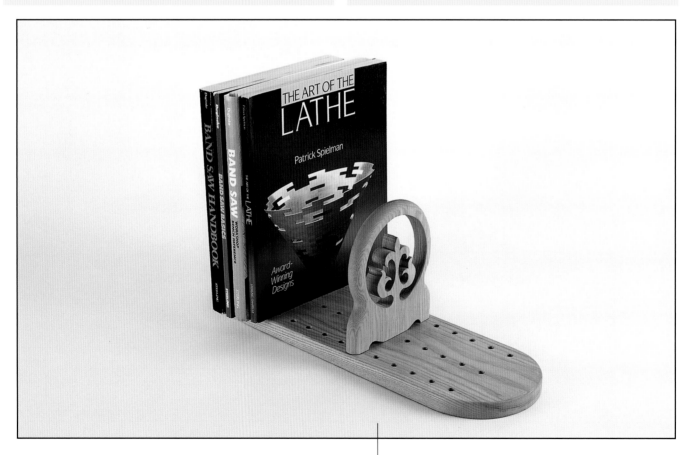

Adjustable Book Ends, oak, 7" high x 9" long x 5¹/₂" wide

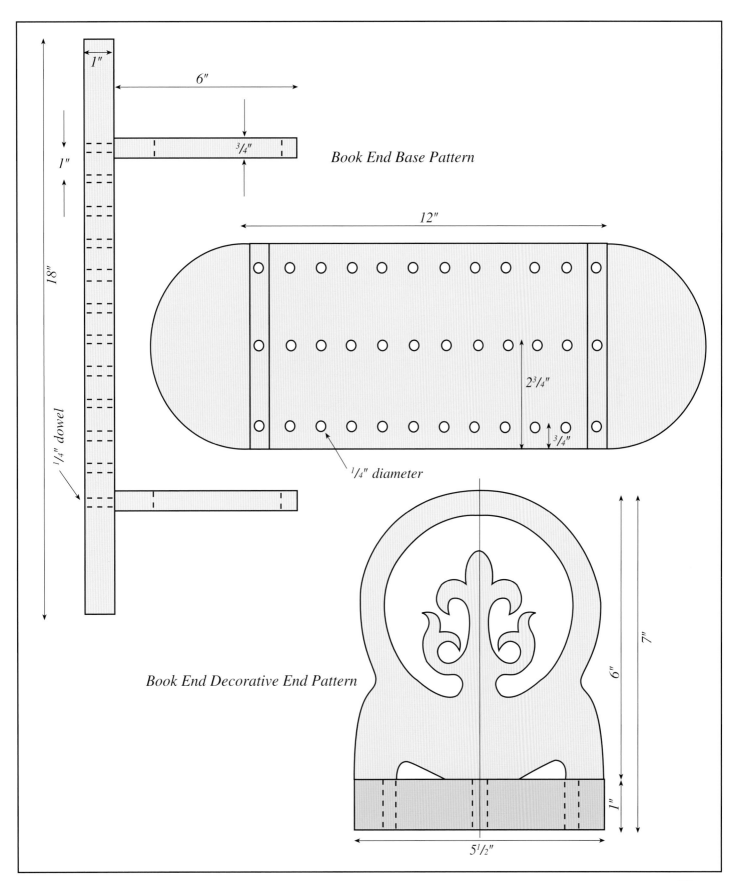

1"

6"

3/4"

Book End Base Pattern

1"

18"

1/4" dowel

12"

2³/4"

³/4"

1/4" diameter

Book End Decorative End Pattern

6"

7"

1"

5¹/2"

77

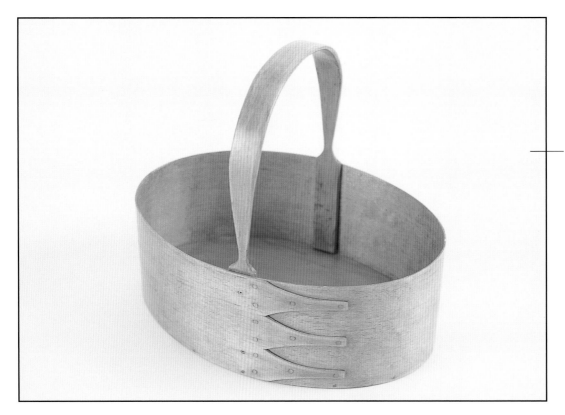

Shaker Basket, yellow birch with a pine bottom, 7" high x 8³/₈" long x 5³/₄" wide

Shaker Basket

Designed by The Shakers

This Shaker basket is made from yellow birch with a pine bottom. It was then stained and varnished.

Shaker baskets or carriers were originally designed to efficiently transport a variety of small items.

They are a study in economical design. For using only a small amount of wood, the design is amazingly strong.

Construction:

1.   Make the pine bottom from wood 8³/₄" long, ¹/₄" thick, and 5³/₄" wide, using the Shaker Basket Bottom Pattern on page 79.

2.   Make the yellow birch side walls from wood 25" long, .060" thick, and 3" wide, using the Shaker Basket Side Wall Pattern on page 79.

3.   Make the yellow birch handle from wood 18" long, ¹/₈" thick, and ³/₄" wide, using the Shaker Basket Handle Pattern on page 79.

4.   Assemble the basket, using rivets.

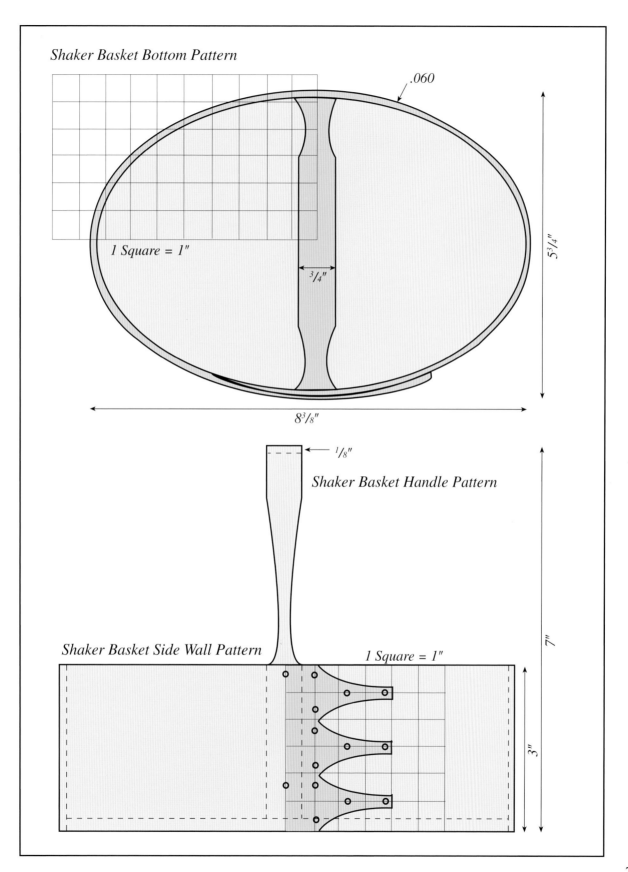

Shaker Basket Bottom Pattern

.060

1 Square = 1"

³/₄"

5³/₄"

8³/₈"

¹/₈"

Shaker Basket Handle Pattern

7"

Shaker Basket Side Wall Pattern

1 Square = 1"

3"

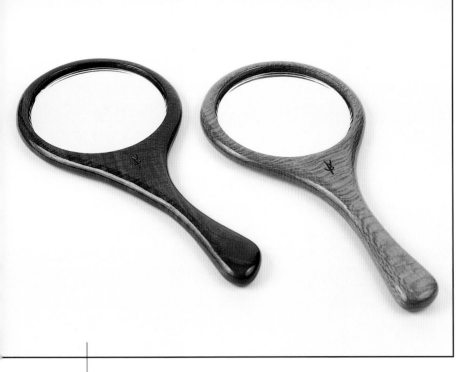

Hand Mirrors, exotic woods, 12¹/₄" long x 6¹/₄" wide x ¹/₂" thick

Hand Mirrors

Designed by Ken Picou

These hand mirrors are made from exotic woods and feature round mirrors.

Oval mirrors can also be used and you can easily change the shape of the handle to suite your taste. It may be a good idea to purchase the mirror first so you can proportion the wood frame to its size and shape.

Construction:

1. Lay the pattern out on the wood, using the Hand Mirror Pattern at right.

2. Rough-cut the hand mirror on the band saw.

3. Make the opening in the hand mirror to accommodate the mirror. The easiest way to make an accurate opening in a piece of wood is with a router bushing set.

Note: If desired, the mirror can be glued directly to the finished wood.

4. Pattern-sand or rout the final edge.

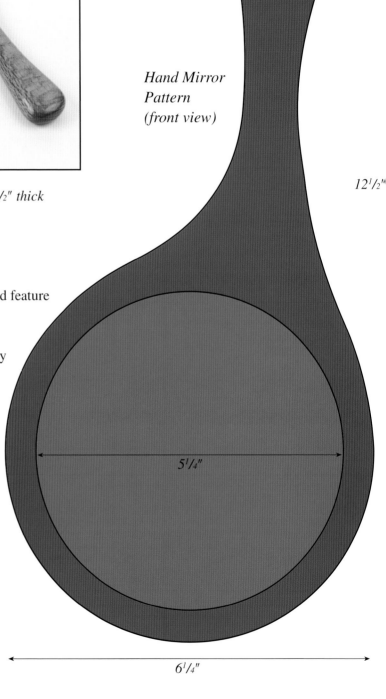

Hand Mirror Pattern (front view)

12¹/₂"

5¹/₄"

6¹/₄"

Train, southern yellow pine, 9" high x 12¹/₂" long x 1¹/₈" thick

Train

Designed by Gus Stefureac

This train is made from construction-grade southern yellow pine. It was then painted with bright colors. The stained carrying case features a briefcase-style handle.

The train is an entertaining toy that is easily transportable. Dowels are used to secure the train inside the carrying case as shown.

Train Carrying Case, southern yellow pine, 12¹/₂" long x 10¹/₂" high x 1¹/₈" thick

Construction:

1.   Make the train engine, cars, and caboose from wood 12¹/₂" long, 1¹/₈" thick, and 9" wide, using the Train Pattern on pages 82–83.

2.   Plane the thickness to 1¹/₈".

3.   Drill the holes in the train engine, cars, and caboose to accommodate the dowels.

4.   Make the wheels with a circle-cutting jig as shown in detail in Chapter 7.

5.   Make the carrying case from three pieces of wood 12¹/₂" long, 1¹/₂" thick, and 9¹/₂" wide, using the Train Carrying Case Pattern on pages 82–83.

6.   Glue the pieces together.

7.   Make the briefcase-style handle from wood 5¹/₂" long, 1" thick, and 1¹/₂" wide, using the Train Carrying Case Pattern on pages 82–83.

8.   Drill the holes in the carrying case to accommodate the dowels.

9.   Assemble the train engine, cars, caboose, and carrying case.

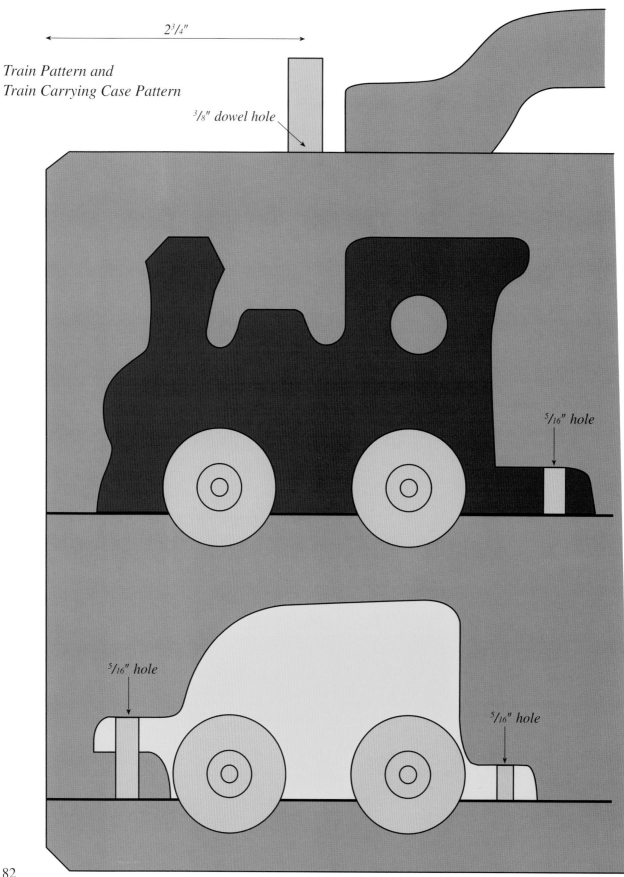

*Train Pattern and
Train Carrying Case Pattern*

2³/₄"

³/₈" dowel hole

⁵/₁₆" hole

⁵/₁₆" hole

⁵/₁₆" hole

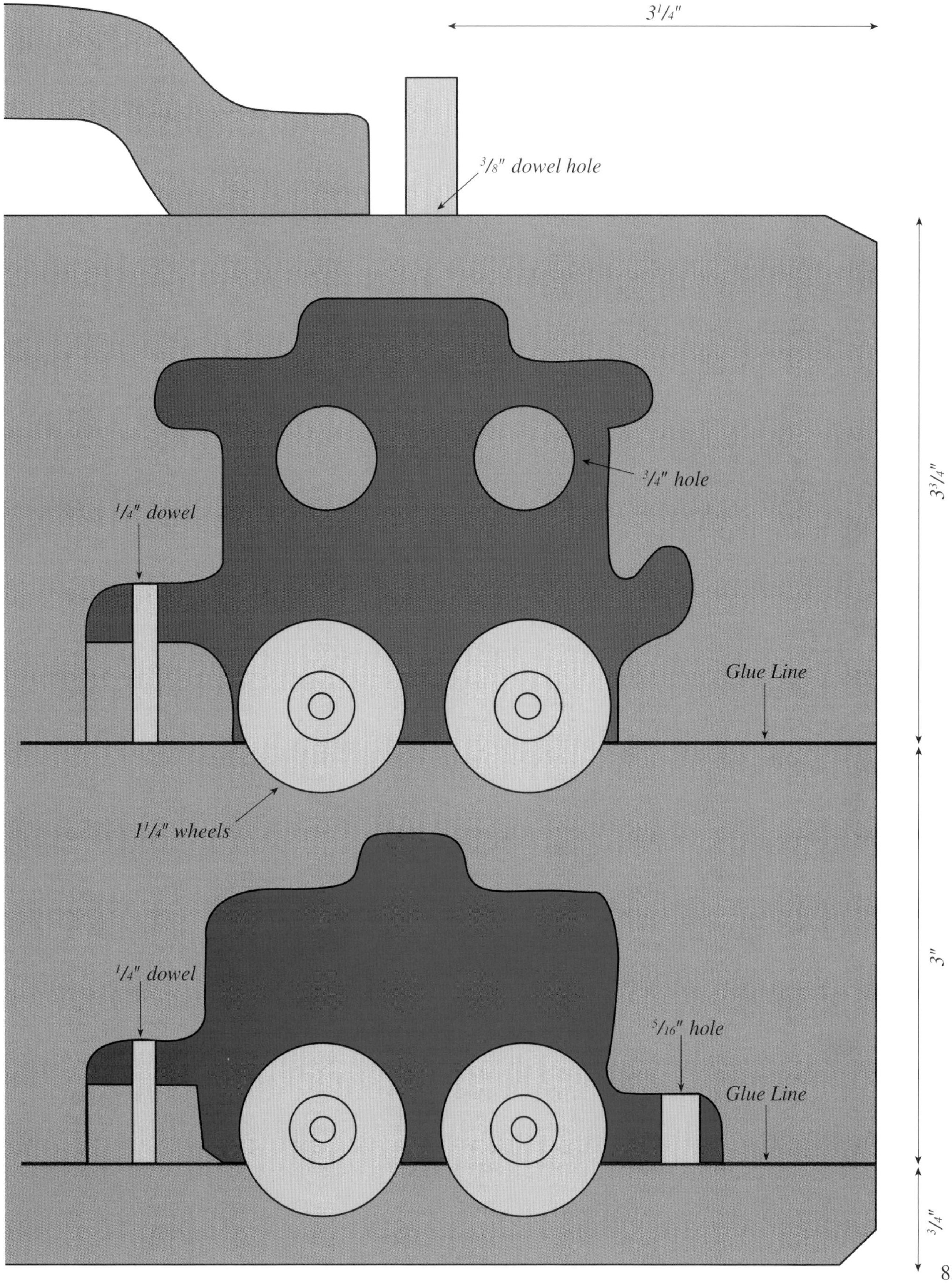

$3^1/4"$

$^3/8"$ dowel hole

$^3/4"$ hole

$^1/4"$ dowel

$3^3/4"$

Glue Line

$1^1/4"$ wheels

$1/4"$ dowel

$3"$

$^5/16"$ hole

Glue Line

$^3/4"$

83

Pickup Truck

From the collection of antique toys belonging to Mary Edwards

This 1930s- or '40s-style pickup truck is made from white pine and then painted. Tin sheeting is used for the running boards and for supporting the front bumper.

Because all of the pieces of wood used to make this pickup truck are curved, it is a perfect band saw project. The design is fairly simple, so it is enhanced by the paint job. The paint is a dull rust red which is similar to an old, faded pickup truck. The black pin-striping, which outlines the doors and hood, adds a nice touch, as does the silver paint on the grill, bumper, lights, and wheels.

Construction:

1.   Make the box sides and the top from wood 10$^{1}/_{2}$" long, $^{3}/_{8}$" thick, and 6$^{1}/_{4}$" wide, using the Pickup Truck Pattern on page 85.

Note: The thin wood can be resawn to thickness.

2.   Make the hood and fenders from wood 10" long, 2" thick, and 6" wide, using the Pickup Truck Pattern on page 85.

3.   Plane the hood and fenders to shape with a sharp block plane.

4.   Make the wheels with a circle-cutting jig as shown in detail in Chapter 7.

5.   Assemble the pickup truck with glue and screws.

Pickup Truck, white pine, 16" long x 6$^{1}/_{8}$" high x 6$^{1}/_{2}$" wide

Pickup Truck Pattern

*Dovetail Box,
cherry,
12" long x
6" high x
5" wide*

Dovetail Box

Designed by Barbara Reif Schneider

This dovetail box is made from cherry and features dovetailed corners and moulded feet.

This decorative box combines a number of band saw techniques, including making the moulded feet for this simple, yet elegant treasure chest. It is a good project for using the band saw dovetail technique as shown in Chapter 8.

The top and the bottom of the box are separated by a seam. One option is to cut the box apart after it has been assembled. The problem with this is that it changes the dovetail spacing. It is best to cut the box top off the box bottom and then tape the two pieces together when cutting the dovetails. Before gluing the box together, remove the tape. This will help maintain the desired dovetail spacing which is important for the look of the finished piece.

If desired, the size of the box can easily be altered to accommodate your treasures.

Construction:

1. Make the box with dovetailed corners from wood 12" long, $1/2$" thick, and 5" wide, using the Dovetail Box Pattern on page 88. This technique is shown in detail in Chapter 8.

2. Make the feet by gluing two mitered pieces of $7/8$" x $7/8$" stock, 2" long. Use a high-quality corner clamp as shown in Illus. 9-3 on opposite page.

3. Clamp the mitered piece to the zero-clearance rip fence on a table saw. Clamp the piece against a flip-stop, then cut the pieces to length as shown in Illus. 9-4 on opposite page.

Note: Both legs of the foot should be cut to the exact length.

4. Make a thin plastic pattern in the shape of the foot, using the Dovetail Box Pattern on page 88 and layout the foot shape on both sides of the foot.

Note: Use a soft-lead pencil or a ballpoint pen because a visible line is crucial. The pattern should be about $1/16$" to $1/8$" from the corner as shown in Illus. 9-5 on opposite page.

Illus. 9-3. The first step in making the feet is gluing two mitered pieces of wood together.

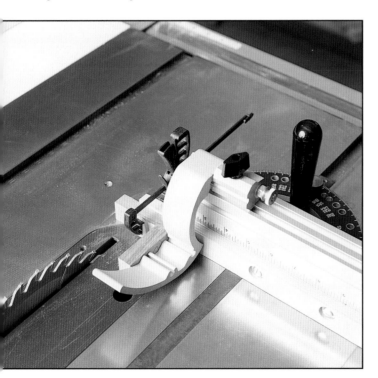

Illus. 9-4. This photograph shows a technique for cutting the mitered piece safely and accurately. The wood is clamped to the zero-clearance rip fence on a table saw. The piece is clamped against a flip-stop, insuring that it will be cut to the exact length.

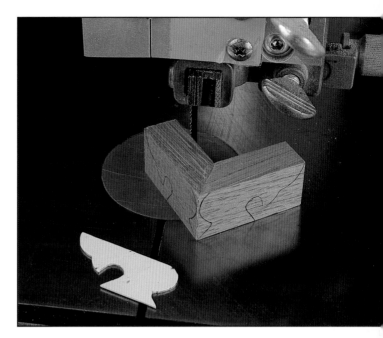

Illus. 9-5. A thin plastic pattern is used to layout the shape on both sides of the foot. The pattern should be about $1/16$" to $1/8$" from the corner.

5. Rather than cutting out the entire pattern, remove the circular element with a drill bit as shown in Illus. 9-6. Use a rip fence to consistently measure the distance between the edge of the board and the hole.

Illus. 9-6. A drill bit is used to remove the circular elements of the pattern. Make certain the workpiece is supported on a piece of scrap, such as a 2 x 4, to keep it from rotating.

6. With a piece of scrap supporting the foot, cut along the line using a ¹/₈" blade. Because the fine-tooth blade is cutting with the grain, the surface will be very smooth as shown in Illus. 9-7.

7. The saw cut will remove the drawn line from the pattern but will expose the end grain of the mating piece, which has exactly the same profile as the original pattern. Rotate the workpiece and make the second cut, creating the curved profile as shown in Illus. 9-8.

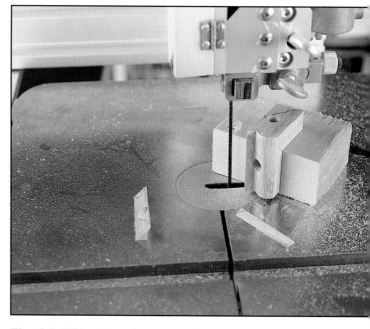

Illus. 9-7. With a piece of scrap supporting the foot, the cut is made with the grain using a ¹/₈" blade. The ¹/₈" blade cutting with the grain leaves a very smooth surface.

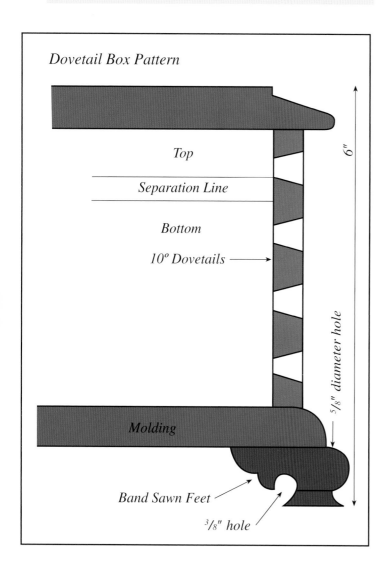

Dovetail Box Pattern

Top

Separation Line

Bottom

10° Dovetails →

6"

⁵/₈" diameter hole

Molding

Band Sawn Feet

³/₈" hole

Illus. 9-8. The completed foot is shown with the exact same profile as the original pattern. The same pattern is shown from both sides.

Checkerboard Box,
checkerboard design of light and dark woods
laminated to walnut, 8" long x 4" wide

Checkerboard Boxes

Designed by Larry Anderson

The first checkerboard box design is laminated to walnut, then cut and reglued with a light veneer strip. The second checkerboard box design features curved lines.

Band saw boxes can be decorated in a number of ways. There is no end to the design variations using these techniques.

Construction:

1. Make the box with checkerboard design from two pieces of wood 8" long, ³/₄" thick, and 4" wide, using the Checkerboard Box #1 Pattern on page 90 or Checkerboard Box #2 Pattern on page 91.

Note: Use dark and light woods, then glue them back together.

2. Make a series of cuts with the two boards fastened together. Use double-sided tape or hot-melt glue to keep the two boards connected to each other during the saw cut.

3. For an interesting design as shown in the photograph above, laminate the checkerboard design to solid stock, then cut and reglue with a light veneer strip.

4. To create the designs shown in the photograph on page 90, cut the pieces, then glue them back together with the wood pieces alternating from dark to light.

Note: The first series of cuts are rip cuts with the grain. The second series of cuts are crosscuts, which create the curved checkerboard design.

Checkerboard Box,
curved checkerboard design of
light and dark woods, 8" long x 4" wide

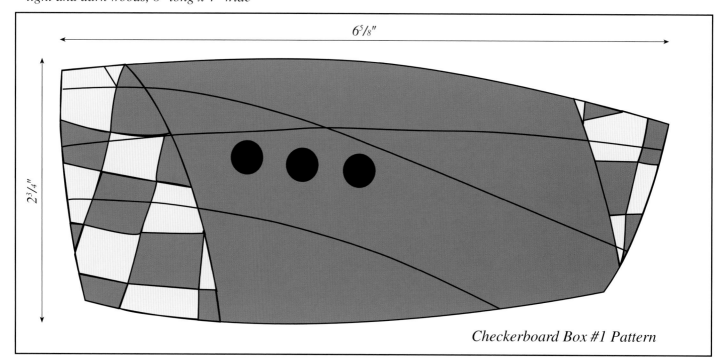

6⁵/₈"

2³/₄"

Checkerboard Box #1 Pattern

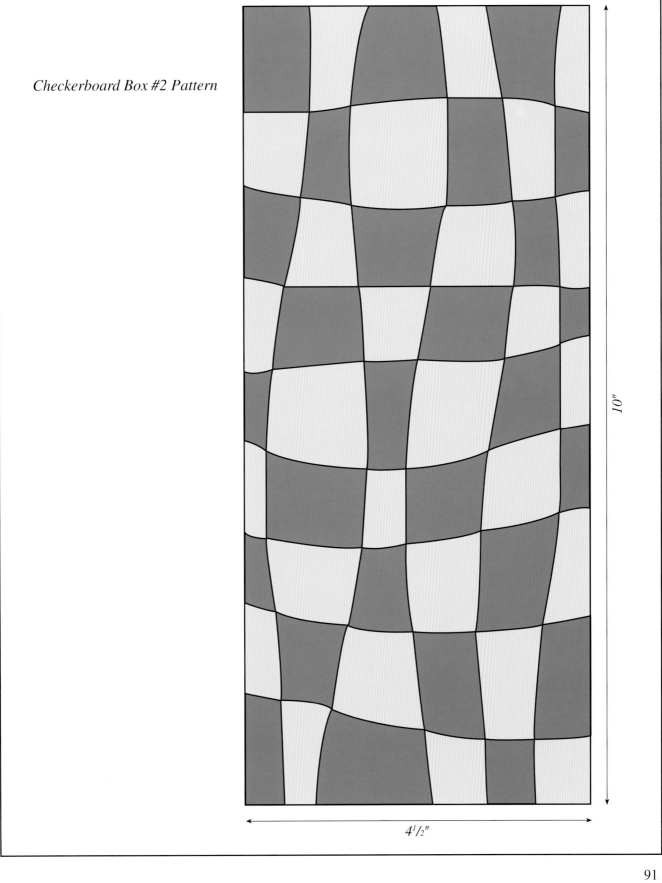

Checkerboard Box #2 Pattern

10"

4¹/₂"

Split-top Box

Designed by Larry Anderson

This split-top box design is a lamination that includes dark and light woods. It features a split-top that is hinged on each corner with a brass pin.

The box is finished on the inside with a dark brown spray-on suede product.

Construction:

1.   Make the box with split-top design from two pieces of wood 8" long and 4" wide, using the Split-top Box Pattern on page 93. The body of the box is 2" thick and the top is ³/₄" thick.

Note: Use dark and light woods. Use the same technique as used in the Checkerboard Boxes on pages 89–91, which will give you two box tops of alternating colors.

2.   Rather than the usual method of making a solid top, make a hinged top. Place a single brass pin in each corner, using the Split-top Box Pattern on page 93.

Split-top Box, maple and cherry, 8" long x 4" wide

Split-top Box, maple and cherry, 8" long x 4" wide Shown open in photograph at left.

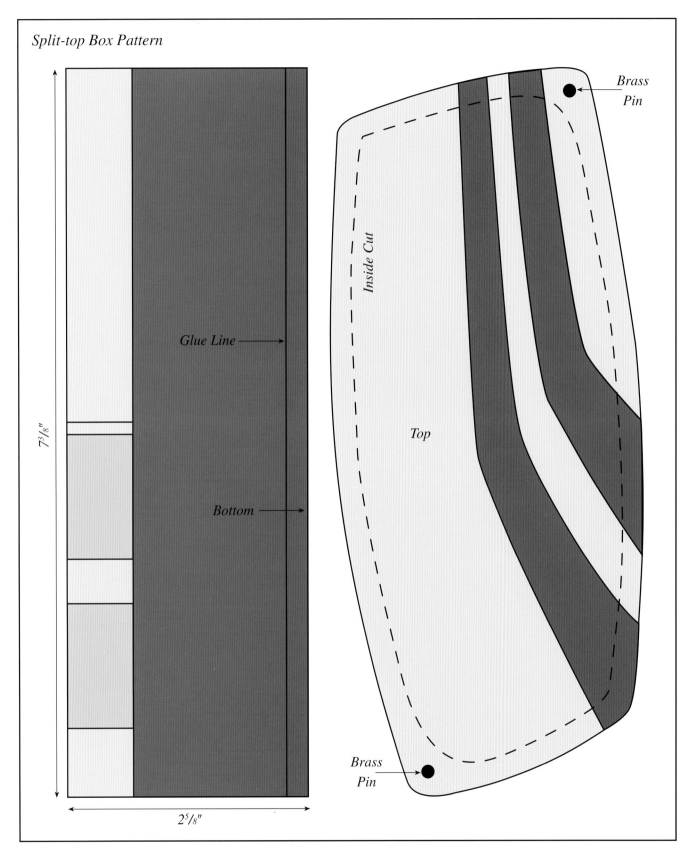

Split-top Box Pattern

Glue Line

Bottom

$7^3/_8"$

$2^5/_8"$

Inside Cut

Brass Pin

Top

Brass Pin

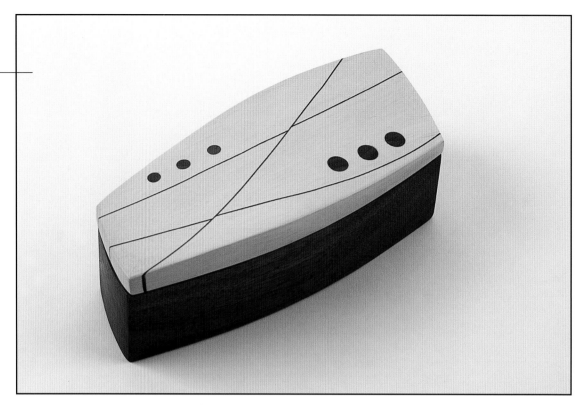

Line & Dot Box,
walnut base
with light top,
8" long x
3¹/₄" wide

Line & Dot Boxes

Designed by Larry Anderson

These line and dot boxes are favorite band saw projects for many woodworkers. It is one way of turning scrap wood into useful items. These boxes can be made from a solid piece of wood or from two different species of wood.

The box in the photograph above has a walnut base and a light top. The top was sawn and then walnut veneer strips were glued in place.

Construction:

1. Make the box with line and dot design from two pieces of wood 8" long and 3¹/₄" wide, using the Line & Dot Box Pattern on page 95. The body of the box is 1³/₄" thick and the top is ³/₄" thick.

2. Cut the opening from the inside of the box, then glue it back together.

Note: The saw cut should be made on the corner of the box, cutting with the grain rather than crosscutting. When the box is glued together, it is almost impossible to see the seam.

3. To make the top and the bottom of the inside of the box, resaw the inside twice.

4. Glue the bottom into the bottom of the box and glue the other piece to the bottom of the top as shown in Illus. 9-9 on opposite page.

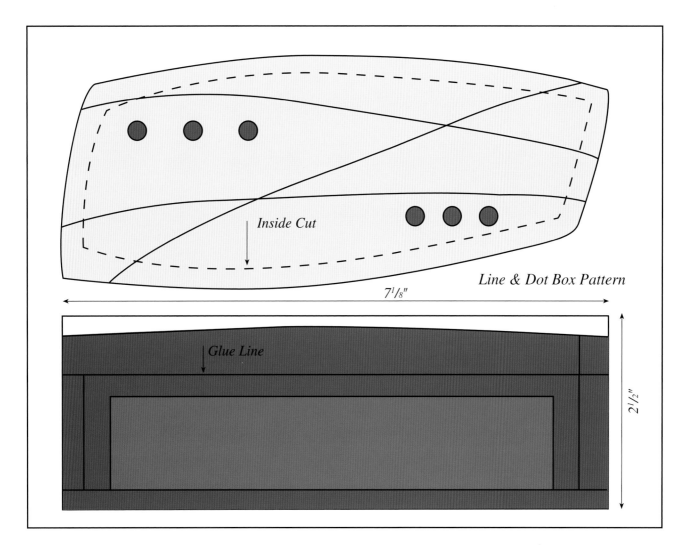

Inside Cut

Line & Dot Box Pattern

7¹/₈"

Glue Line

2¹/₂"

Illus. 9-9.
The inside is usually resawn twice to make the top and the box bottom. One piece is glued into the bottom of the box and the other piece is glued to the bottom of the top.

95

Moon Face Tables,
cherry and maple,
22" high x 18" diameter

Moon Face Tables

Designed by Jeffrey L. Kurka

These tables challenge one's woodworking skills with the band saw and the router. The maple and cherry tabletops are cut in half and then matched with the opposite pieces to form the face of the "man in the moon" on the edge of the seam.

The curved legs complement the round tabletop and the curves of the face.

The process of jointing two pieces of wood with a curved line is a technique that can be intimidating. Like any other acquired skill, understanding the process and experimentation with scrap wood is a good idea.

Construction:

1. To make the tabletops, use two pieces of wood (one piece of maple and one piece of cherry) 20" long, $^3/4$" thick, and 14" wide, using the Moon Face Tabletop Pattern on page 98.

Note: Because the tabletop is 18" wide, the pattern needs to be at least 19" long. The pattern is then cut along the profile line with a $^1/8$" blade. The smaller blade allows for tighter curves, creating a sharper pattern.

2. Cut the tabletops in half along the face pattern line.

3. Clamp the appropriate template to the top of the tabletop and trim the edge with a router and a guide bushing set as shown in Illus. 9-10.

4. Rest the guide bushing against the template and very accurately trim the saw cut. Trim the mating piece with the mating template to produce a perfect match.

Note: When it is glued together, the glue line is almost invisible.

5. To make the table legs, use three pieces of wood (cherry) 36" long, $^3/4$" thick, and 4" wide, using the Moon Face Table Leg Pattern on page 98.

Note: The legs consist of three pieces that are glued together with dowels.

6. Until the glue has dried, temporarily clamp the pieces together with glue or screw tabs.

7. Make the central column from 2 x 2 stock, 17" long.

8. Attach the legs to a central column as indicated on the Moon Face Table Leg Pattern.

Note: Another option is to cut the mating sides at 30° and glue the legs directly to each other. The outside edge of each leg would then be rounded with a radius bit to give it a smooth continuous shape.

9. To add the stars in the tabletops, make a template first, then rout them in or carve them.

Note: The star is filled with clear acrylic epoxy.

Illus. 9-10. The tabletops are cut in half along the face pattern line. The appropriate template is then clamped to the top of the tabletop and the edge is trimmed with a router and a guide bushing set. When the two halves are glued together, the glue line is almost invisible.

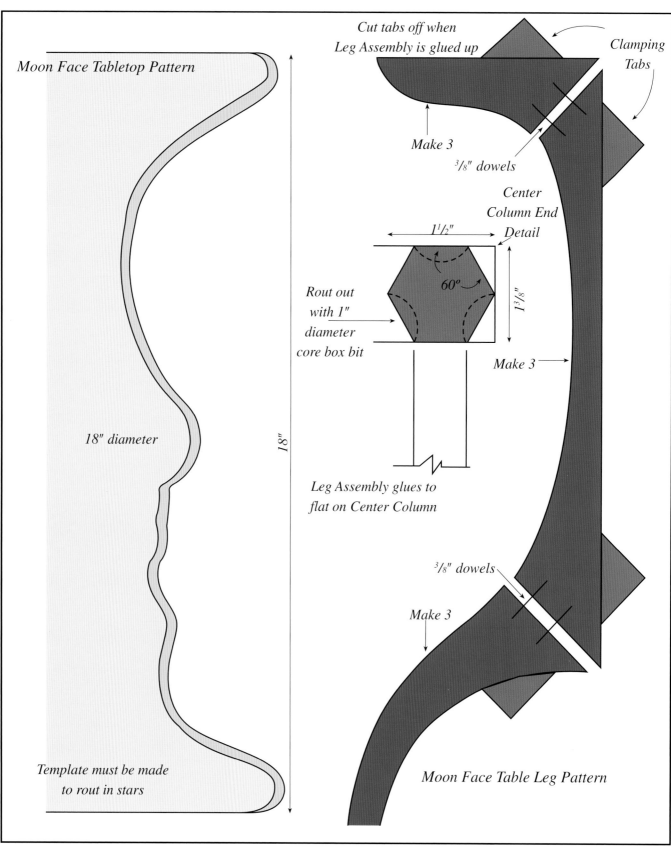

Moon Face Tabletop Pattern

18" diameter

18"

Template must be made
to rout in stars

Cut tabs off when
Leg Assembly is glued up

Clamping
Tabs

Make 3

$^3/_8$" dowels

Center
Column End
Detail

$1^1/_2$"

Rout out
with 1"
diameter
core box bit

60°

$1^3/_8$"

Make 3

Leg Assembly glues to
flat on Center Column

$^3/_8$" dowels

Make 3

Moon Face Table Leg Pattern

Kentucky Table, cherry,
28³/4" high x 36" long x 18" wide,
construction instructions on page 100

Kentucky Table

Designed by Warren May

This table is made from cherry and its design requires a band saw to make the cabriole legs and the curved apron.

A characteristic of Appalachian and French Canadian furniture is the use of European design elements, such as the cabriole leg. The designs are simplified and thinner pieces of wood are used on these table legs.

This leg design is a good use of optical illusion in furniture design because the leg appears to be made from a bigger piece of wood than is actually used.

Construction:

1. To make the tabletop, use one piece of wood 36" long, ³/₄" thick, and 16" wide, using the Kentucky Tabletop Pattern at right.

Note: The tabletop has a 1" overhang.

2. Rout the edges of the tabletop with a flush-trimming router bit.

3. To make the apron, use one piece of wood 31" long, ³/₄" thick, and 6¹/₄" wide, using the Kentucky Table Apron Pattern at right.

4. To make the cabriole legs, use four pieces of 2 x 2 stock, 28" long, using the Kentucky Table Leg Pattern at right.

5. Rotate each leg so the apron end is a 45° angle as it is jointed to each leg.

Note: The traditional way of jointing the apron to the leg is with a mortise and tenon joint. For the less ambitious, a biscuit joint would work.

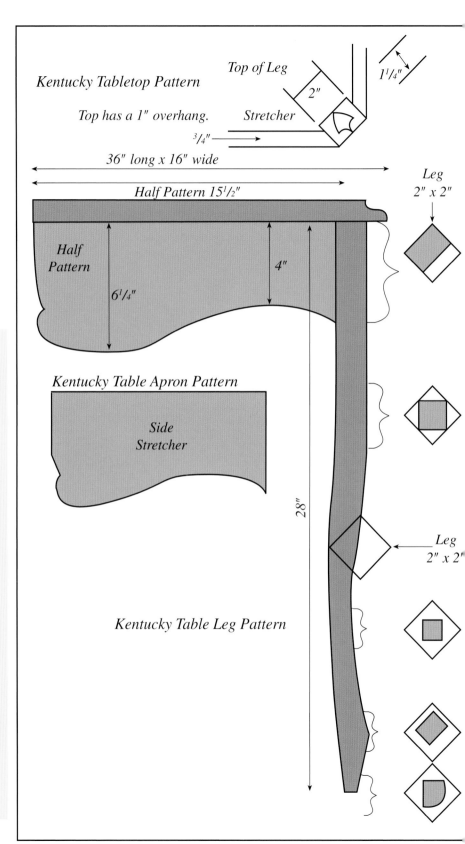

Kentucky Tabletop Pattern

Top of Leg

Top has a 1" overhang. Stretcher

1¹/₄"

2"

³/₄"

36" long x 16" wide

Leg 2" x 2"

Half Pattern 15¹/₂"

Half Pattern

4"

6¹/₄"

Kentucky Table Apron Pattern

Side Stretcher

28"

Leg 2" x 2"

Kentucky Table Leg Pattern

Demilune Tables, bird's-eye maple, cherry, and bubinga,
29³/4" high x 30" long x 13" wide,
construction instructions on page 102

Demilune Tables

Designed by Fal Wing

These tables are made from bird's-eye maple, cherry, and bubinga. The contrasting colors juxtaposed against the same shape make an interesting statement.

They feature legs that have been tapered on all four sides and the "balls" give the tabletops a light feeling, as if they were floating. The straight aprons offer a sharp contrast to the semicircular tabletops and are partially the reason why these tables have such a unique design.

The grain of the wood is accentuated with a clear finish, allowing the light to reflect off all three tables from the same location.

Construction for one table:

1.   To make the tabletop, use one piece of wood 30" long, $^3/_4$" thick, and 13" wide, using the Demilune Tabletop Pattern on page 103.

2.   To make the apron, use one piece of wood 24$^3/_4$" long, $^3/_4$" thick, and 2$^1/_2$" wide, using the Demilune Table Apron Pattern on page 103.

3.   To make the legs, use three pieces of 2$^1/_2$" x 2$^1/_2$" stock, 26$^1/_2$" long, using the Demilune Table Leg Pattern on page 103.

Note: The three legs are identical and are tapered on all four sides.

4.   Make the balls 2$^1/_2$" in diameter.

5.   Use traditional joinery throughout.

Demilune Tables, bird's-eye maple, cherry, and bubinga, 30" long x 29$^3/_4$" high x 13" wide

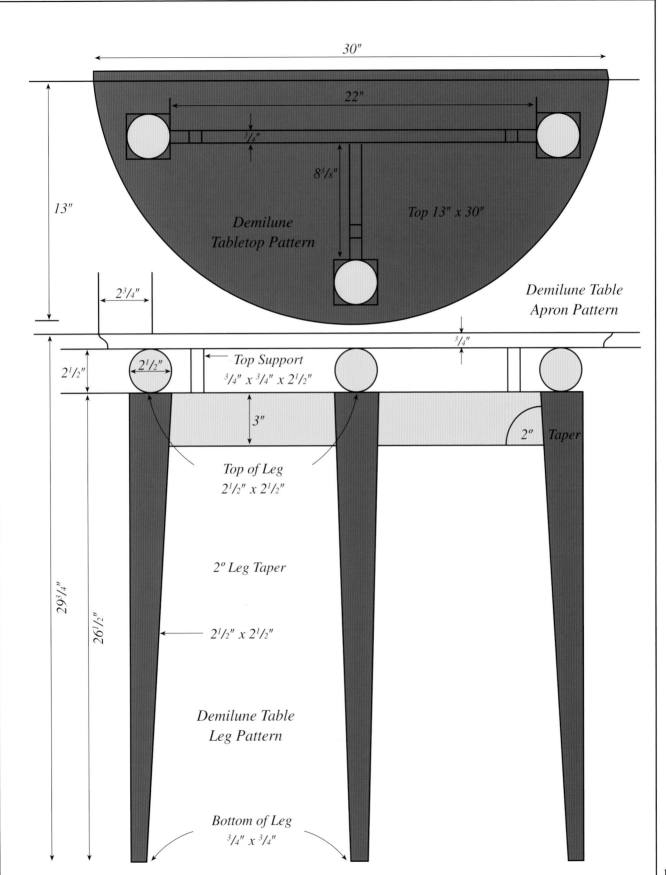

30"

22"

³/4"

8³/8"

Top 13" x 30"

13"

Demilune
Tabletop Pattern

Demilune Table
Apron Pattern

2³/4"

³/4"

2¹/2"

Top Support
³/4" x ³/4" x 2¹/2"

2¹/2"

3"

2° Taper

Top of Leg
2¹/2" x 2¹/2"

2° Leg Taper

29³/4"

26¹/2"

2¹/2" x 2¹/2"

Demilune Table
Leg Pattern

Bottom of Leg
³/4" x ³/4"

103

*Maple Chair,
maple,
32" high x
17³/₈" wide x
16³/₁₆" deep*

Maple Chair

Designed by Mark Duginske

Most woodworkers agree that the most difficult piece of furniture to make is a chair. This chair is designed to complement a number of different furniture styles. When made in maple, cherry, or walnut, it goes well with Shaker designs. When made in oak with a few slight variations, it goes easily in a room with Arts & Crafts designs.

We recommend a good working knowledge of the previous chapters in this book. Chapter 6 shows in detail how to make a curved top back slat.

Construction:

1. To make the back chair legs, use two pieces of wood 32" long, $^7/_8$" thick, and 4" wide, using the illustrations provided on this page and on pages 106–111. To make the front chair legs, use two pieces of $^7/_8$" x $^7/_8$" stock, $17^3/_4$" long.

2. Drill holes at 90° with a drill press to accommodate the dowels between the two front chair legs.

3. Fit the dowels and the chair backs into the back legs parallel to each other, making the mortising and drilling simple.

Note: The front and the back legs are parallel to each other. The stretchers between the front and the back leg are also parallel to each other and at 90° angles to the front legs. Refer to the top, front, and side views as shown.

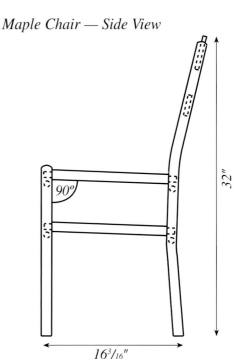

Maple Chair — Side View

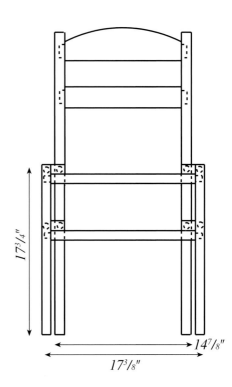

Maple Chair — Front View

Maple Chair — Top View

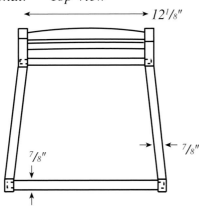

105

4. Make certain the back legs are shorter than the front legs so the chair angles back slightly.

Note: The distance between the floor and the bottom dowels holding the legs together is different on the front and back legs. The distance between the floor and the bottom dowel on the front legs is 10$\frac{1}{4}$"; the distance on the back legs is only 10" as shown below.

5. You will need to make two back legs. To do this efficiently and to guarantee the size, make a jig to do the final shaping on the router table. This technique is shown in detail in Chapter 7.

Note: The top and the bottom of the chair legs are angled back from the middle of the chair. The shape of the back leg curve is shown at right and on opposite page.

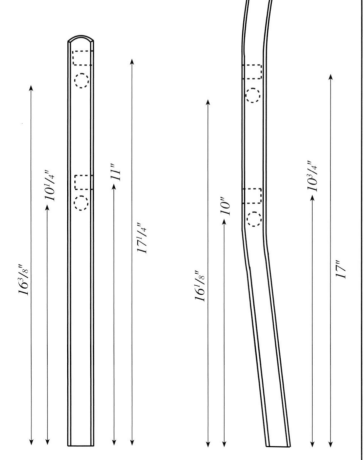

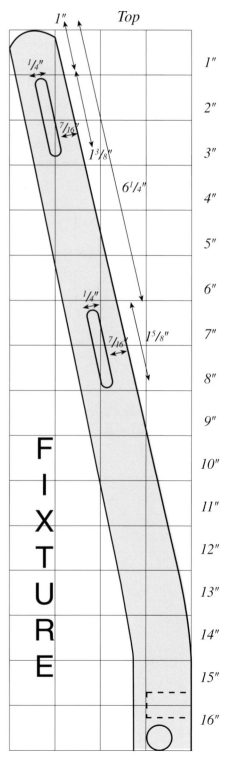

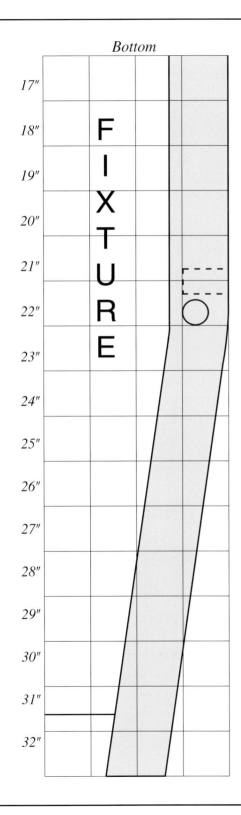

Bottom

17"
18"
19"
20"
21"
22"
23"
24"
25"
26"
27"
28"
29"
30"
31"
32"

FIXTURE

6. Rough-cut the workpiece on the band saw, then clamp it to a fixture that has an edge with the shape of the pattern.

Note: The fixture with the shape of the pattern contacts the bearing of the router bit as shown below.

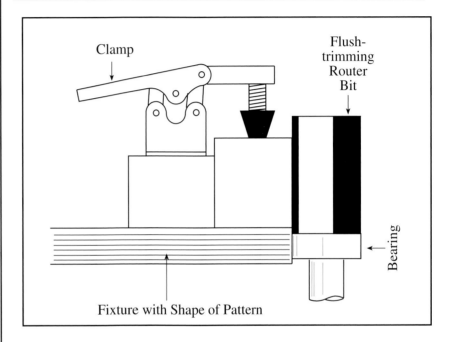

Clamp

Flush-trimming Router Bit

Bearing

Fixture with Shape of Pattern

7. Remove any material that is proud of the pattern with the flush-trimming bearing, leaving a chair part that is exactly the size of the pattern.

8. Secure the chair legs to each other with square stretchers that are trimmed on the ends to create round dowels. This can either be done with a drill press and a dowel cutter or a lathe.

Note: The dowels are fit into the holes drilled in the chair as shown in detail on page 106.

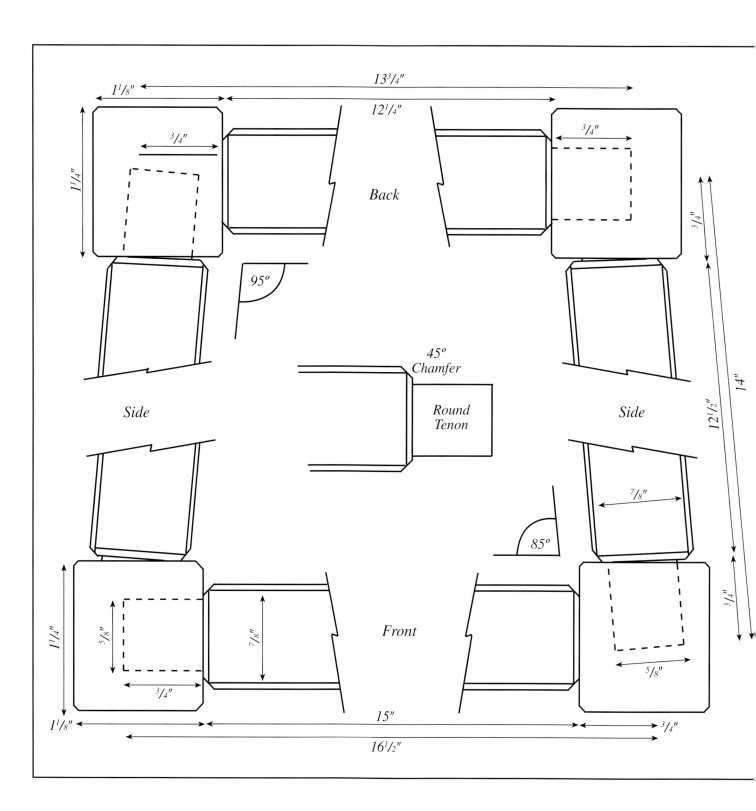

9. Trim the stretchers on all four corners with a 45° router bit.

10. Make the dowels with a drill press and a dowel cutter or a lathe.

Note: The dowels that fit into the legs are $7/8$" long. The dowel cutter is very efficient at making the round shape, but it leaves a rough edge at the end of the cut. By trimming the corner with the blade tilted at 45° as shown at right, the rough edge is eliminated.

11. Angle the stretchers between the front and back legs at 5°, then drill a hole in the legs at 5° to accommodate the dowels on the end of the stretcher.

Note: A 5° angled platform that fits on your drill press will support the leg for the drilling operation as shown below.

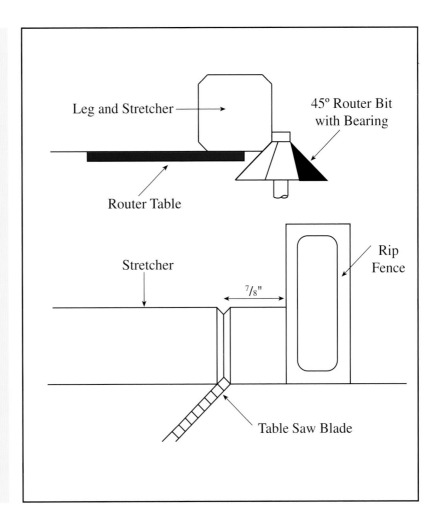

Leg and Stretcher

45° Router Bit with Bearing

Router Table

Stretcher

$7/8$"

Rip Fence

Table Saw Blade

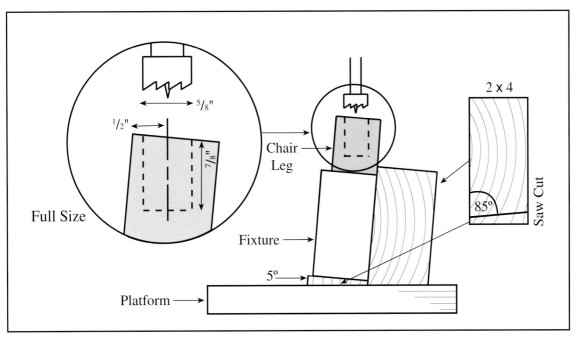

Full Size

$5/8$"

$1/2$"

$7/8$"

Chair Leg

Fixture

5°

Platform

2 x 4

85°

Saw Cut

12. Make the curved chair back. This technique is shown in detail in Chapter 6.

Note: Refer to the illustrations of the mortise and tenon joint for the chair back, the detail of the curved chair back, and the detail of the curved chair back and the tenon as shown below and on opposite page.

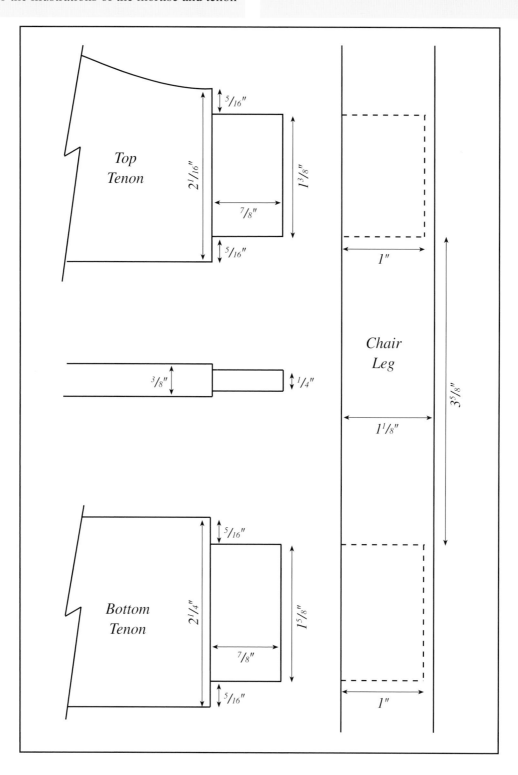

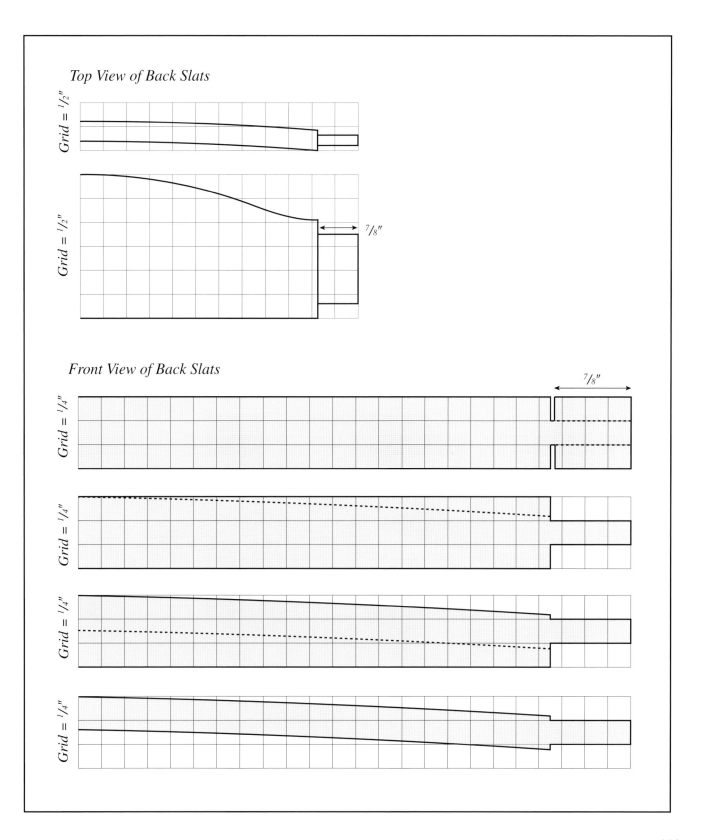

Top View of Back Slats

Grid = ¹/₂"

Grid = ¹/₂"

⁷/₈"

Front View of Back Slats

⁷/₈"

Grid = ¹/₄"

Grid = ¹/₄"

Grid = ¹/₄"

Grid = ¹/₄"

Oak Arts & Crafts Chair, *red oak with* *walnut slats,* *35" high x* *18" wide x* *18" deep*

Oak Arts & Crafts Chair

Designed by Jeffrey L. Kurka

This chair is a variation on an Arts & Crafts design. The chair is made of red oak with walnut slats.

Most woodworkers agree that the most difficult piece of furniture to make is a chair. However, this particular chair is designed to make it easier to construct than most chairs. The simple, straightforward lines of Arts & Crafts movement were a reaction to the excesses of the Victorian era.

This type of design also lends itself well to machine production.

We recommend a good working knowledge of Chapters 6 & 8 before beginning this project, as well as an overview of the Maple Chair on pages 104–111.

Construction:

1. To make this chair, use four pieces of wood 38" long, 2" thick, and 7" wide using the illustrations provided on this page and on pages 114–115.

2. You will need to make two front legs. To do this efficiently and to guarantee the size, make a jig to do the final shaping on the router table. This technique is shown in detail in Chapter 7.

Note: Repeat the process and the technique to make the two back legs as shown at right.

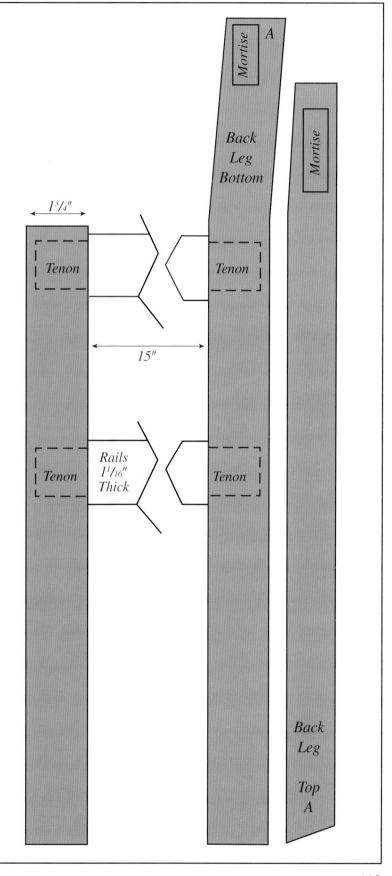

3.   Rough-cut the workpiece on the band saw, then clamp it to a fixture that has an edge with the shape of the pattern.

Note: The fixture with the shape of the pattern contacts the bearing of the router bit.

4.   Remove any material that is proud of the pattern with the flush-trimming bearing, leaving a chair part that is exactly the size of the pattern.

5.   Secure the chair legs to each other with rectangular stretchers that have a tenon on each end.

Note: The tenons fit into the mortise in the chair legs as shown below.

6.   Make the curved chair back. This technique is shown in detail in Chapter 6.

Note: The curved chair back is mortised and tenoned into the back chair legs. The walnut slats are mortised and tenoned into the curved chair back. Refer to the drawing of the mortise and tenon slats for the curved chair back as shown below.

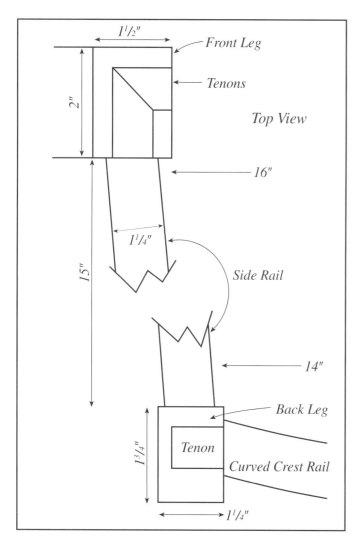

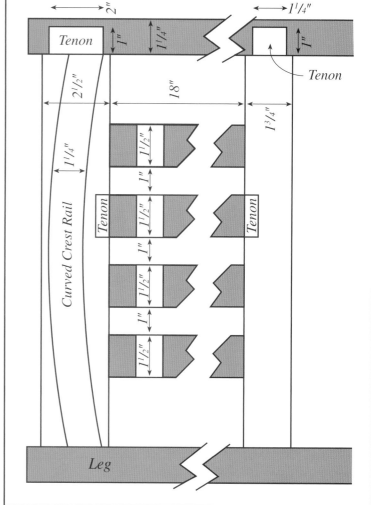

CHAPTER 10

artists' gallery

"Caduceus"
Clothespress
by Noel Swanson,
walnut with
cherry highlights,
92" high x
22" wide x
19" deep

Photo: Popular Front Photography

115

Miniature Animals by Steve Tomashek,
basswood painted with acrylic paint, approximately 3" high

Fire Engine Jewelry Box by Dwight Speh,
walnut and maple, 6" high x 18" long x 5" wide

Stool by Glenn Gordon,
ash, wenge, and hickory,
24^1/$_2$" high x 14" wide x 17" deep

Stool by Glenn Gordon,
white ash,
26" high x 14" wide x 14" deep

118

Stool by Glenn Gordon,
Swiss pear with metal foot ring,
28" high x 14" wide x 14" deep

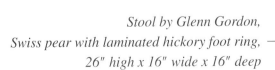

Stool by Glenn Gordon,
Swiss pear with laminated hickory foot ring,
26" high x 16" wide x 16" deep

Stool by
Glenn Gordon,
cocobolo seat,
25" high x
14" wide x
14" deep

Spindle Prairie Chair by Ron Betcher,
white oak, 28" high x 42^1/$_2$" wide x 37^3/$_4$" deep

Photo: Popular Front Photography

*Dressing Mirror
by Ric Allison,
kwila,
72" high x
27" wide x
13" deep*

Wooden-geared Clock
by Dwight Speh,
cherry,
84″ high x
18″ wide x
10″ deep

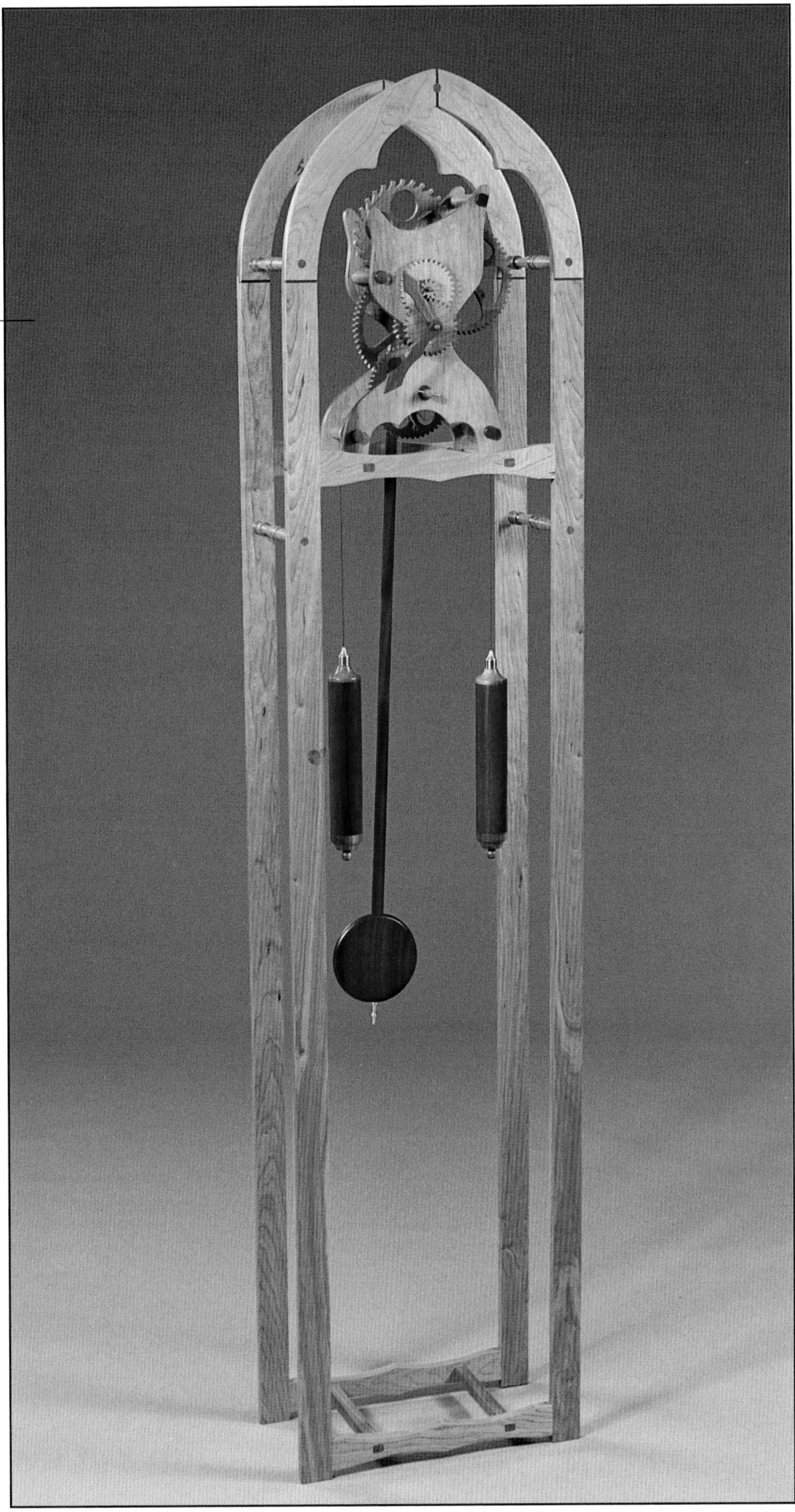
Photo: Popular Front Photography

Single-drawer Shaker Sewing Table by Richard Gotz,
bird's-eye maple, 28" high x 21" wide x 18" deep

Artemus Dresser Chest by Donald Grandbois, curly maple, 60" high x 32" wide x 20" deep

*Display Table
by Nick Clark,
kwila,
19" high x
10" diameter*

*Display Table
by Yeung Chan,
doussie,
36" high x
18" wide x
18" deep*

Guitar
by John Bogdanowicz,
East Indian rosewood
and Western cedar,
39$^{1}/_{2}''$ high x
14$^{1}/_{2}''$ wide x
5'' deep

*Suspended Vessel
by Craig Lossing,
maple burl,
cocobolo,
and ebony,
12" high x
6" wide x
3" deep*

*Rocker
by Jeff Miller,
maple,
41" high x
25" wide x
41" deep*

130

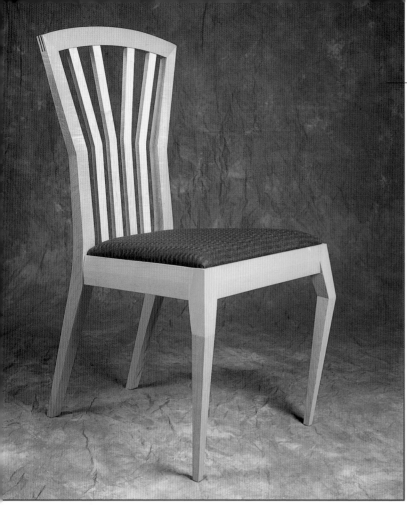

*Spider Chair
by Jeff Miller,
maple,
36" high x 20" wide x 21" deep*

*Neoclassical Chair by Jeff Miller,
mahogany, 35" high x 19^1/$_2$" wide x 21" deep*

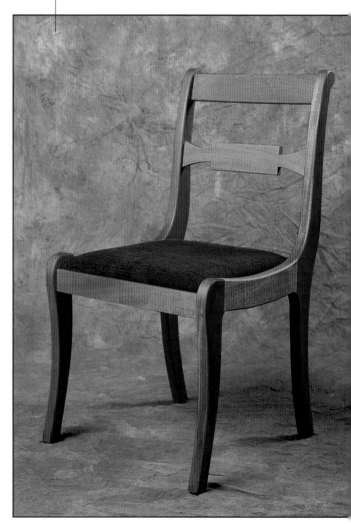

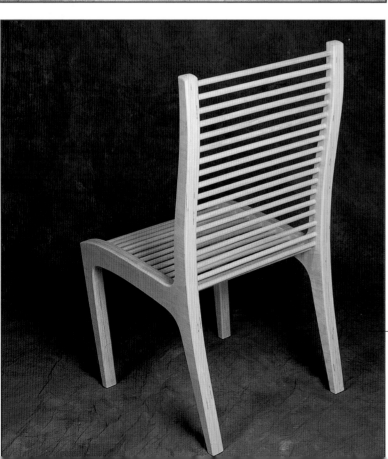

*Dowel Chair
by Jeff Miller,
maple,
37" high x 19" wide x 20^1/$_2$" deep*

*China Cabinet
by Tomás Moreno,
bibilo and kwila,
60" high x
24" wide x
20" deep*

"Fat Boy" by Jari-Pekka Vilkman,
mahogany, 54" high x 44" wide x 8" deep

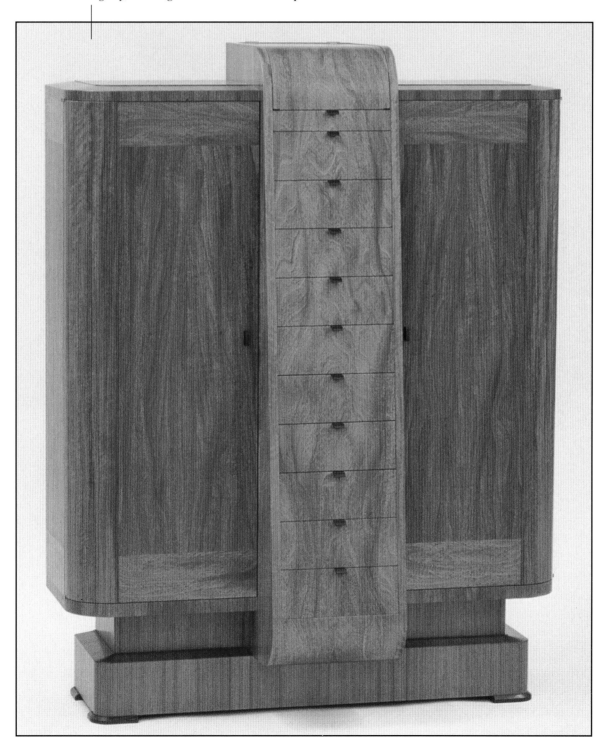

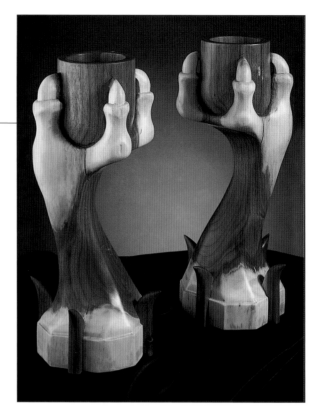

Dragon Chalices
by Keith Trier,
black walnut heartwood
and sapwood,
cups 4" diameter;
16" high x 7" wide x 7" deep

Tansu Box
by Cindy Park,
elm,
9" high x 25" wide x 9" deep

Chickadee Cabinet
by Craig Vandall Stevens,
Norway maple
and white oak,
52" high x
25" wide x
17" deep

135

*Spider Handkerchief Table
by Jeff Miller,
purpleheart and
bird's-eye maple,
30" high x
45" wide x
22$\frac{1}{2}$" deep x
32" square with
the leaf up*

*Arts & Crafts Hallway Table
by Paul Leinbach,
quarter-sawn white oak
with white marble top,
30" high x 54" long x 16" deep*

Photo: Popular Front Photography

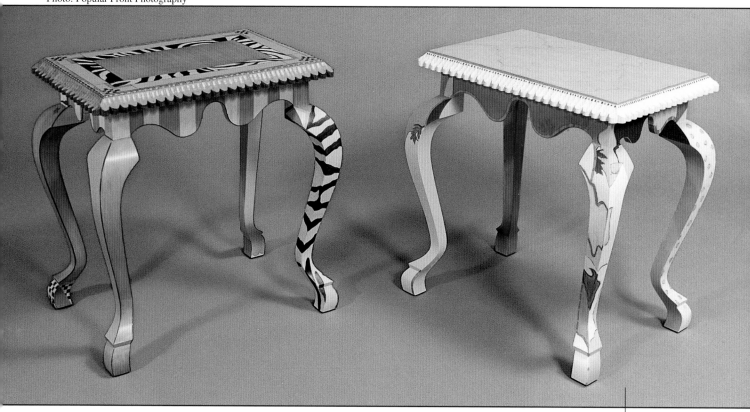

End Tables by K. Libbey Nash and Robert and Terry Kinghorn, MDF and miscellaneous hardwoods with painted surfaces, 27" high x 26" long x 18" deep

Triangular Table by David J. Marks, Brazilian ipe wood with fossilized ivory inlay, 25" high x 20" wide x 48" long

Photo: Don Russel

Armchair after Vidar Malmasten by Vajra Ricchi,
hickory, 33" high x 20¹/₂" wide x 15³/₄" deep

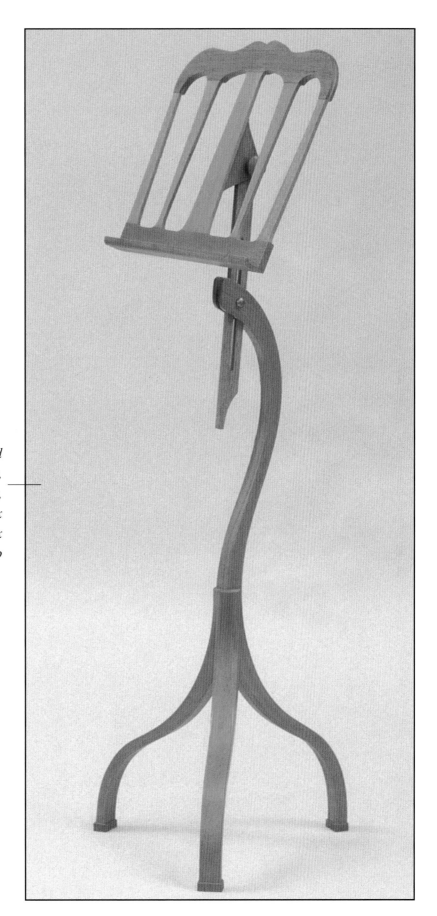

*Music Stand
by Elisabeth Darragh Perrow,
mahogany,
50" high x
19" wide x
15" deep*

*Queen Anne
Bonnet Top
Highboy by
Tom VanBinsbergen,
tiger maple,
82" high x
38" wide x
18" deep*

*Dining Table
with Built-in
Trivet by
Elizabeth Barnard,
figured cherry,
33" high x
30" wide x
80" long*

*Blanket Chest
by Don Wattenhofer,
black walnut,
24" high x
20" wide x
60" long*

*Display Cabinet
by Greg Smith,
pear,
20³/₄" high x
12" wide x
8" deep*

*Jewelry Cabinet by
Nina Childs Johnson,
mahogany and
Western maple,
13" high x
18" wide x
9" deep*

metric conversions

INCHES TO MILLIMETRES AND CENTIMETRES

MM-Millimetres   CM-Centimetres

INCHES	MM	CM	INCHES	CM	INCHES	CM
$1/8$	3	0.9	9	22.9	30	76.2
$1/4$	6	0.6	10	25.4	31	78.7
$3/8$	10	1.0	11	27.9	32	81.3
$1/2$	13	1.3	12	30.5	33	83.8
$5/8$	16	1.6	13	33.0	34	86.4
$3/4$	19	1.9	14	35.6	35	88.9
$7/8$	22	2.2	15	38.1	36	91.4
1	25	2.5	16	40.6	37	94.0
$1^1/4$	32	3.2	17	43.2	38	96.5
$1^1/2$	38	3.8	18	45.7	39	99.1
$1^3/4$	44	4.4	19	48.3	40	101.6
2	51	5.1	20	50.8	41	104.1
$2^1/2$	64	6.4	21	53.3	42	106.7
3	76	7.6	22	55.9	43	109.2
$3^1/2$	89	8.9	23	58.4	44	111.8
4	102	10.2	24	61.0	45	114.3
$4^1/2$	114	11.4	25	63.5	46	116.8
5	127	12.7	26	66.0	47	119.4
6	152	15.2	27	68.6	48	121.9
7	178	17.8	28	71.1	49	124.5
8	203	20.3	29	73.7	50	127.0

YARDS TO METRES

YARDS	METRES	YARDS	METRES	YARDS	METRES	YARDS	METRES	YARDS	METRES
$1/8$	0.11	$2^1/8$	1.94	$4^1/8$	3.77	$6^1/8$	5.60	$8^1/8$	7.43
$1/4$	0.23	$2^1/4$	2.06	$4^1/4$	3.89	$6^1/4$	5.72	$8^1/4$	7.54
$3/8$	0.34	$2^3/8$	2.17	$4^3/8$	4.00	$6^3/8$	5.83	$8^3/8$	7.66
$1/2$	0.46	$2^1/2$	2.29	$4^1/2$	4.11	$6^1/2$	5.94	$8^1/2$	7.77
$5/8$	0.57	$2^5/8$	2.40	$4^5/8$	4.23	$6^5/8$	6.06	$8^5/8$	7.89
$3/4$	0.69	$2^3/4$	2.51	$4^3/4$	4.34	$6^3/4$	6.17	$8^3/4$	8.00
$7/8$	0.80	$2^7/8$	2.63	$4^7/8$	4.46	$6^7/8$	6.29	$8^7/8$	8.12
1	0.91	3	2.74	5	4.57	7	6.40	9	8.23
$1^1/8$	1.03	$3^1/8$	2.86	$5^1/8$	4.69	$7^1/8$	6.52	$9^1/8$	8.34
$1^1/4$	1.14	$3^1/4$	2.97	$5^1/4$	4.80	$7^1/4$	6.63	$9^1/4$	8.46
$1^3/8$	1.26	$3^3/8$	3.09	$5^3/8$	4.91	$7^3/8$	6.74	$9^3/8$	8.57
$1^1/2$	1.37	$3^1/2$	3.20	$5^1/2$	5.03	$7^1/2$	6.86	$9^1/2$	8.69
$1^5/8$	1.49	$3^5/8$	3.31	$5^5/8$	5.14	$7^5/8$	6.97	$9^5/8$	8.80
$1^3/4$	1.60	$3^3/4$	3.43	$5^3/4$	5.26	$7^3/4$	7.09	$9^3/4$	8.92
$1^7/8$	1.71	$3^7/8$	3.54	$5^7/8$	5.37	$7^7/8$	7.20	$9^7/8$	9.03
2	1.83	4	3.66	6	5.49	8	7.32	10	9.14

index